Everything you need for your Exhibitions, Presentations and Promotions... is right under one roof at

PHOTOBITION

London Tel: 01-736 1331 • Bristol Tel: (0272) 427105/423426 • Cardiff Tel: (0222) 463681

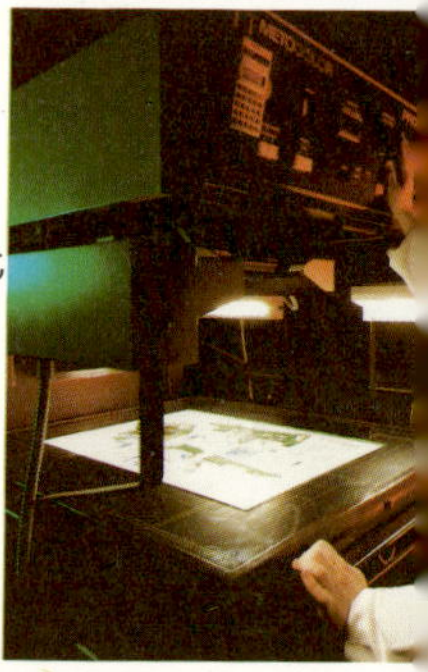

Call in to your nearest Photobition and you will find the answer to virtually every graphic or photographic requirement you can think of.

Including Computer Graphics, Exhibition Display Graphics, Colour and Black and White enlarging, and Modular Display Systems and Accessories.

The fullest use is always made of the latest technology and techniques for producing Typesetting, Artwork, Photographic Processing, Mounting, Silk Screening and Litho Printing. But truly amazing is the scope offered by our high resolution Computer Graphics whereby graphs, bar charts and pie charts can be acheived in the shortest possible time. Photobition has branches in London, Bristol and Cardiff.

A **Daily Telegraph**
BUSINESS ENTERPRISE BOOK

HOW TO SET UP & RUN CONFERENCES & MEETINGS

Published by Telegraph Publications
135 Fleet Street, London EC4P 4BL

© Telegraph Publications/William Curtis Publishing 1986

This book is sold subject to the condition that it shall not, by way of trade or otherwise, be lent, resold, hired out or otherwise circulated without the publisher's prior consent in any form of binding or cover other than that in which it is published.

All rights reserved. No part of this work may be reproduced or transmitted by any means without prior permission of the publisher.

Whilst every care has been taken to ensure the accuracy of the contents of this work, no responsibility for loss occasioned to any person acting or refraining from action as a result of any statement in it can be accepted by the publisher.

ISBN 0 86367 096 2 paperback
0 86367 101 2 hardback

British Library Cataloguing in Publication Data

How to set up and run conferences and meetings
1. Congresses and conventions
658.4'562   AS6

Typeset by Rowland Phototypesetting Ltd, Bury St Edmunds
Printed by Biddles Ltd, Guildford and King's Lynn

A **Daily Telegraph**
BUSINESS ENTERPRISE BOOK

HOW TO SET UP & RUN CONFERENCES & MEETINGS

THE CONTRIBUTORS

We would like to express our appreciation of the help given by the following contributors in the preparation of this book.

Audio Visual Presentation Advisory Service
Barbara Cox
Meetings World Group Limited

Terry Pottinger
Moorgate Group plc

Marlene Garsia
series editor

Geoffrey Gray-Forton
consultant

Case studies were contributed by:

Peter Battam
world marketing services manager, Jaguar Cars Ltd

Tony Carey
chairman of the Guernsey chapter, ACE International

Tom Davy
sales director, Kogan Page Ltd

Anthea Fortescue
managing director, Conference Associates Ltd

Sarah Henley
pr/sales executive, Sari Fabrics Ltd

Fred Wakefield
president, International Congress and Convention Association

Judy Whittam
conference organiser, The Institution of Agricultural Engineers

Andrew Williamson
conference manager, University of Newcastle upon Tyne

CONSULTATIVE PANEL

Association of British Professional Conference Organisers (ABPCO)
Anthea and Tim Fortescue

Association of Conference Executives (ACE International)
John Farrer

Audio Visual Presentation Advisory Service
David Coupe and Peter Kane

British Association of Conference Towns (BACT)
F. Lloyd McLean

Conference Managers Association
Derek Pace

Hotel Industry Marketing Group (HIMG)
Andrew Bryne

International Congress and Convention Association (ICCA)
Dev Anand and Fred Wakefield

Contents

Preface vii

1 Setting the objectives 1
   Sales meetings 6
   Promotional meetings 7
   Educational or trade seminars 8
   Training courses 9
   Press conferences 9
   Incentive conventions 10

2 Budgeting for a conference 19
   Those often forgotten costs 24
   Cash flow forecast 26

3 The programme 30
   Other conference content 34

4 The importance of selecting a suitable venue 40
   Understanding your needs 43
   What to look for when selecting a venue 43
   The site visit 45

5 Choosing the right audio visual medium 56
   Getting it right 62
   How are AV programmes made 64
   Facilities 69
   The use of AV in conferences 73
   Facts and figures 75

6 How to hold an audience's attention 81
   Planning your speech 85
   Different methods of presentation 89
   Guest speakers 92
   Rehearsals 93

7 Further planning considerations 95
   Conference timetable 97
   Pre-conference literature 100
   Travel and accommodation 103
   Secretarial and administrative assistance 104

    Translation and interpretation   105
    Equipment hire   105
    Venue point   106
    Security   108
    Extras   109

8 Conference catering   112
    Different types of catering   114

9 Planning a conference abroad   122
    Potential problems   128
    D-Day   132

10 Introducing exhibitions   134
    Security   141
    Stand staff   142
    A calendar of key dates   144

11 Has it been a success?   148

Appendix I   A selection of conference venue sites   168

Appendix II   Other useful addresses   173

Appendix III Associations   177

Index   181

The contributors   183

Preface

Organising conferences or meetings for the non-professional organiser can turn into a painful learning experience, exposing a number of hidden problems. This is not to cast any doubts on your own ability, but after all, you are a professional in another sphere and your expertise lies in other areas. It could be that this is the first time you have organised a conference or meeting. More than likely, you have attended a number of company meetings and as a result, have developed an awareness of the specific requirements which are needed in order to produce a successful event.

It is because of the vast difference between being a mere participant and on the other hand shouldering the responsibility of organising a conference or meeting, that this comprehensive handbook was conceived and published.

Conferences are a key way in which companies and institutions communicate with their staff, members and the outside world. Mistakes in organising these events can be costly and embarrassing, and can seriously tarnish people's perception of how well an organisation is run.

As companies become more aware of the need to improve communications (both internally and externally) on a cost-effective basis, the delegation of responsibility in organising conferences or meetings plays an increasingly important role. As these meetings tend to be held infrequently, perhaps with intervals of six months or more, so it is difficult to build up the experience necessary to ensure that everything runs trouble-free.

Noting all these points, it became clear that executives and their assistants needed a practical working guide which went through all the stages of organising a meeting. Essential for a book of this sort were check lists – not only reminders of all basic tasks but those often unthought of ones too. Organising a conference or meeting also necessitates a degree of creativity of presentation, hence a number of hints have been included. Appendices at the end of the book include names and addresses of venues, conference organisers and other useful sources of information.

The content of this title, in common with the rest of the series, relied on consultations with and contributions from professional organisers, senior executives of associations and institutions, all with many years of experience in the conference industry. Support in the form of relevant Case Studies has been given by companies, institutions, associations and a university – to all we express our gratitude.

How to Set Up and Run Conferences and Meetings is a step-by-step guide through the logistics of planning and conducting a successful conference or meeting. As such, it complements the existing range of books published by Telegraph Publications in supplying comprehensive, practical advice.

1 Setting the objectives

The types of seminars, conferences, meetings and presentations you may need to arrange can be extremely varied, ranging from small intimate gatherings to full scale presentations involving very large audiences. It may involve your own staff or sales force, and often require you to talk to people you do not know. The object of your meeting may be to put over specific information (press conferences, staff meetings, product launches, etc.) or it may be an incentive or reward style of meeting (sales conventions). Deciding the type of meeting and its purpose is your very first step.

Although the purpose of the meetings may vary, you will need the same basic approach. Conferences, in whatever form, can be the most efficient way of putting a message over, often to a very large number of people, in a very short period of time; but if badly organised, they can be disastrous. Staged for the wrong reason, at the wrong time, with the wrong content, to the wrong people, they not only become a financial 'Titanic' (often with the same loss of 'life' – particularly the organisers!) but the company's image or morale can be irreparably damaged. But what, you may ask, can be done to avoid this happening? The key thing to do *before anything else*, is to define very carefully why you need the meeting. Ask yourself whether you need it at all? And what do you want the meeting to achieve?

One thing you should not overlook when considering the type or style of your company's future meeting, is to decide very carefully whether it will stand alone or be part of a wider method of putting across the same message. Do you need printed material to supplement it? (Almost invariably you will.) Do you need to run an advertising campaign? Do you need a series of smaller meetings or lunches to 'spread the word'? (This will depend on the purpose of your meeting.)

During these initial and all-important stages, you and your colleagues will be discussing the type, objectives, and style of your company's conference or meeting. It is very important at this stage to develop clear lines of communication. Far better now to thoroughly discuss your colleagues' views rather than be blamed later for mishandling things. Define very carefully the objective of the meeting and the audience you want to reach. Once this is done, you can move on to the content, venue and the budget – the latter element can be either the most important or the most restricting one. The conference budget is discussed in detail in Chapter 2.

But let us first go back and examine the objective, what is it? Is it information or incentive? Perhaps it is a product launch or party? Or perhaps reinforcement or reward? And who will your audience be? People from outside your company or members of staff? Before you leap into action, take the time to sit down and carefully ask yourself (and answer!) a series of questions. Make sure you know why you are running the meeting and what the objective is. If you do not know what you want to achieve before you start, and how to put it across, the chances are your audience will not know either once you have finished.

A lot of people in the conference business have come

1 SETTING THE OBJECTIVES

up with a list of questions to help define the organisational needs of a conference. You can probably come up with your own, but the following may help.

1. Who do I want to talk to?
2. What do I want to say?
3. When do I say it?
4. Where do I say it?
5. Why do I want to say it?
6. How do I say it?

Once the questions have been answered, you are on the way. The next thing to do is work on the content and the style. But be careful here. It is very easy to decide the content first and then let the content decide the objective. Obviously whilst the two are inter-related, you must know the object *before* you decide on the content. The content is there to achieve the objective *not* to determine it!

So, what about the content? What do you need to worry about? The two main areas here are the verbal and the visual content. The two are inter-linked and should work together. Do not rely too heavily on one or the other. Always remember who the audience is, what the message is, and who is delivering the message. Input here from colleagues can be of great assistance, so do not be afraid to ask. If it is a sales meeting ask your sales director, or if it is a promotional launch ask your marketing director. Certainly, if you are part of a small committee, discussion will be invaluable.

As well as being informative, perhaps persuasive, the meeting needs to be entertaining and the content must reflect this need. Remember people's level of concentration is more limited than you expect (or they admit). So the meeting needs to allow for that. Whether it is a short, sharp 30 minute presentation or a one or two day meeting, your audience needs to remain interested in your message; this is the only way that you can successfully ensure that most of the information is retained.

Depending on the type of meeting, one of the most successful ways of building up the interest, and the reinforcement of the message, is to run a theme throughout the meeting. This can take many forms and can be used very effectively in all pre or post meeting printed material. It also helps in defining exactly what the various speakers say or what the form of the presentation is. It can also create a memorable image for the whole meeting by following this theme through in areas such as set design, speaker support, printed material and even colour schemes. Whether it is the more common theme of 'Winner's' or 'Challenge' or 'The Future', or the more esoteric themes such as 'The Inner Man' or 'Human Capabilities', a theme can add a more solid base to the meeting, tying in both the visual and the verbal content in helping to achieve the objective.

Do not, however, fall into the trap of working out a clever theme for a conference if it does not need one. Again, it is very much dependent upon the message and the audience – and if you are not careful, you may get so involved in trying to maintain a particular theme, that you get away from your original objective. Recently I was invited to a one day conference that had as its theme 'Winning', the purpose of which was to motivate and inspire a sales force to greater efforts. The problem was, however, that the conference was so full of top flight athletes and footballers giving pep talks, and included so many slides and films on sporting winners, that it finished up more like a six-hour advertisement for the Sports Aid Council or the Football League.

So the vital areas that you have to remember when organising a meeting is to define very carefully on the outset, the following:

1. The objective.
2. The theme and content.
3. The budget.

After that brief introduction to the conference world generally, what are the various types of conferences,

Scotland is renowned for the vast and breathtaking wilderness that makes up its "great outdoors".

Indoors, however, its style has for a long time been rather cramped. With few indoor spectator venues of any reasonable size worth speaking of.

Until the Scottish Exhibition+Conference Centre came along, that is.

The creation of this £36m multi-purpose venue means that, for sporting events Scotland is a whole new ball game.

Its five halls offer spacious accommodation from 775 up to 10,000 square metres. From standing room for 3,600 people or a massive seating capacity of 10,000 in the largest hall, to a smaller audience of 2,000 in a sound-proofed and air-conditioned conference auditorium. Whilst the overall clear height throughout all the halls is 9m, Halls 4 and 5 have high bay areas with clear heights of 20m and 14m.

As a highly flexible venue, the SECC also has unrivalled technical facilities. A sophisticated underfloor network of walkways and trenches carries water and waste pipes, mains electricity and telephone cables to manholes at 10 metre intervals.

Come to Scotland for the wide open spaces.

And 5.5 metre high, 6 metre wide doors allow easy access for equipment trucks. Overall, the Centre is geared to accommodate fast outside broadcast set-up time in the halls, requiring little or no additional camera lighting.

As you can see, all these features make the SECC ideal for indoor sports ranging from tennis and gymnastics up to six-a-side soccer and show jumping.

Another big advantage of the Centre is its location. The SECC stands at the heart of a highly efficient motorway, rail and air network only minutes from the centre of Glasgow. The airport itself is only 12 minutes away and there are 21 flights to and from London each day.

The SECC serves a market which spends 20% more than the UK average on theatre and sporting events, and which has almost a million people aged between 15 and 25 living within one hour's travelling distance.

Next time you're searching for a venue, think big.

Contact Carl Martin, Sales Manager – Events, Scottish Exhibition+Conference Centre, Glasgow G3 8YW. Telephone 041-248 3000.

Scottish Exhibition+ Conference Centre

meetings or seminars that you may need to organise. Listed on the following pages are the more common types, together with some points that may need to be considered for each one.

Sales meetings

Most sales meetings are a combination of information (*actual* results and targets) and motivation (*better* results and *achievement* of targets). Which of the two is the more important? Or are they equally important? Is the audience your own sales force or are you talking to independent intermediaries? When is the best time to talk to them? Is there a particular time of the year when they would be more receptive than others? Will they be worried about a meeting that cuts into their selling time – or more concerned about one that disrupts their personal life?

Sales meetings by their very nature, tend to contain a lot of numbers. Sales targets, year end results by branch, results by region or by national or international areas; results compared to last year; individual or branch results; profits; budgets; the list goes on, and each point is equally important. So make sure that they are put across in a way that is easily digested and understood by the audience. Use visual aids such as 35mm slides; overhead projectors; flip charts to support the theme. Always remember, however, that these aids are intended to be support for the speaker and *not* to make him redundant. (See Chapter 5 on Choosing the right audio visual medium.)

If you are throwing a lot of information at the audience, do not forget to mix it up a bit and include sections that also entertain. Do not be afraid to use humour to maintain interest and to *help motivate*. Do not forget that a sales force (yours or an independent one) is a vital element in the success of your company (some would say *the* vital element!) so any presentation to them has to reflect this.

It is very important that your content be informative, entertaining, professional and reinforce

1 SETTING THE OBJECTIVES

the message, in their minds, of their importance to you.

Promotional meetings

In most instances, these meetings will be the vehicle to promote (or launch) your product, either to the potential buyers or to the people who sell it for you – the company's own sales force or independent operators who you wish to influence.

Here the objective is very clear and really defines itself. The content, therefore, is very much the product. What it is, what it does, how it works, how much it costs and why people should buy it. This does, of course, lend particular possibilities for a theme to be used.

For a promotion such as this, it may be that you need a series of meetings around the country (or abroad, see Chapter 9). If so, you need to consider carefully the methods used to present the show. Do not go overboard on equipment if it means three ten-ton lorries have to go to twenty venues to talk to twenty-five people at each, see if there is an easier way of doing it.

The other area which becomes important here if you are talking to the public or sales people other than your own, is the invitation. Who is going to be invited? How do you invite them? What would make them want to come to the meeting? (They may get quite a few invitations to meetings such as yours.) How do you find the people to invite?

If you are promoting a particular product, you are at the same time promoting your company. That may sound rather obvious, but many people do not fully recognise this fact. So again, be professional, create the right image and do not over elaborate the presentation. Always bear in mind that many people remember the product by the *meeting* they went to and not necessarily the fine detail of the product itself.

Educational or trade seminars If you are involved in setting up this type of meeting, it probably means that you will be going to people outside your organisation and inviting them to attend an 'association' type of meeting. These can take many forms and be aimed at different levels or groups of expertise in different fields. The time taken will tend to cover two or three days and involve various presentations by different speakers. Here your problems of organisation could be rather diverse. Will it involve international travel? Do you have to make sure that you have enough bedrooms (of the right quality) for the delegates? How do you find the right speakers? Do you need to find sponsors for the meetings? Are you selling tickets for delegates to attend (with or without their partners)? Have you got to set up a separate accounting system? Have you got to worry about arranging optional local tours or trips for partners (or delegates) not attending specific sections of the meeting? Do you need space in the hotel (or conference site) for a small exhibition? Do you need separate syndicate rooms? Do you need to arrange conference dinners and invite after-dinner speakers or cabaret?

As indicated above, the range of areas to consider may be wide when organising this type of meeting; however, the presentations and speakers require similar thought and decision as discussed at the beginning of this chapter.

This is an area where themes can lend themselves very nicely to enforcing the message. It may be that you are running a seminar for people of similar professions, albeit they are self-employed (doctors, dentists, small one-man businesses). The purpose of the meeting may be to discuss certain legislation or proposed legislation. It may be that you wish to announce or endorse the advantages of an association to members. Think very carefully of the objectives of the meeting, and whether or not a theme will enhance the message.

1 SETTING THE OBJECTIVES

Training courses

If you are arranging training courses they will tend to be for your company's own staff and the content is probably more easy to define. You, and the personnel manager, need to give careful thought to the location and facilities. It is important that delegates can both learn and relax in a conducive atmosphere. If the course is being run at the company's offices, do not arrange accommodation for people in a hotel 20 miles away. If there is not a good hotel nearby, take the course to the hotel (assuming, of course, that they have got proper facilities!).

Give delegates enough time to absorb the training and for private study. Make sure you have also allowed time for them to relax. (Does the hotel have a swimming pool, a snooker room, squash courts, a solarium – and a bar that stays open late?)

Mix up the speakers and the presentations. If you have got some heavy sessions, follow them with something a little more lighthearted (a simple quiz or some type of group game or competition). Use film or video to create different types of presentations. Get all speakers to use flip charts or overhead projectors to create interest. Allow plenty of time for delegates to ask questions at the regular review sessions held at the beginning or end of each day. Make sure all reading material (or supporting literature) is understandable and is available on time with enough copies for everybody.

Press conferences

It may be necessary at some stage to arrange a press conference. In many ways you should consider this as another promotional meeting, though obviously bearing in mind your audience. Do not be overawed purely because you are talking to the press: always remember that members of the press are normal human beings.

Obviously the purpose of a press conference is to obtain press coverage for your company and its product(s) or service(s), and if you put a good story over well to the press they will respond positively. Remember that they are looking for interesting and worthwhile pieces of news to include in their columns.

Invitations to press launches are therefore crucial. It is no good inviting the sports journalist of your local paper to come along to a presentation for a brand new all-singing, all-dancing electric robot (although with some football teams in mind that may not be a bad idea!). You need to know which journalist covers the specific field which you are presenting to. It may be that you also need to arrange a series of press lunches to get to know certain journalists more intimately (and for them to get to know you) prior to your press conference.

The conference itself should be kept as factual and informative as possible with the minimum of frills. Whilst it may be helpful to have a number of supporting visual aids, your presentation will normally be in the form of a prepared presentation by key personnel followed by (no more than three or four and for five minutes each) a question and answer session and then by lunch (over which you can talk to, and be questioned by, the journalists). Make sure you have an information pack for each journalist, re-confirming all the points made at the conference. A press release is important and should be sent to those papers who do not send a journalist along to the meeting, but only send it on the day of the event (or a few days before with an 'Embargo' note on it so that it will not be printed until the specified date).

Incentive conventions

It may be that you have to organise a sales convention for your sales force as an incentive for sales results. This would normally involve overseas hotels and venues, although not necessarily. Consider choosing sites where the field force would not generally go to as individuals. Arrange matters so that during the convention delegates participate in things which they would not normally do. The launch of an incentive convention needs to be forceful and maintain

*Heritage Centre,
The World's Largest
Working Steam Engine,
Waterbus Service,
Concert Hall,
Exhibition Centre,
Canalside Walks,
Picnic Gardens,
Education Centre,
Working Machinery Hall,
Gift Shop and Information,
Pub and Restaurant.*

CONFERENCE CENTRE

Wigan Pier, Lancashire WN3 4EU
Telephone: (0942) 323666

momentum (bearing in mind that the conventions normally are held at the end of a predetermined 'sales period'). Use a full range of marketing ploys, or aids, to build interest and maximise attendance.

Overseas conventions (be they incentive or for other reasons) often lend themselves to themes which can be used to great effect, so consider very carefully if you have a particular objective or theme which can be enhanced by a particular venue (or vice versa).

If a convention is being offered as a reward for results, it must reflect the efforts made by the attendees. Make them feel important. Remember that conventions such as this should not only be a 'reward' but should be seen as a marvellous method of creating or building company morale and image.

We have briefly run through the more common types of conferences although, of course, your own particular meeting may be a combination or variation, of the above. Whatever the type of meeting, just sit down before you start and think the whole thing through and define exactly what you want. A lot of the points for consideration, or areas to organise, will be similar no matter what the meeting is, and are often just a case of using common sense.

We mentioned before the importance of a conference committee; it may be that you need to set up an organising committee although this must be done with the purpose of delegating responsibilities or tasks *not* to abrogate them. Do not take on too much if the task of organising the meeting is particularly time consuming, complicated or short of lead-in time. There is nothing worse than accepting too heavy a load and compromising the result. Get people to help, but always keep your finger on the pulse. Remember you are responsible. It is no good taking the attitude, 'If it goes well, *I* did it – if it goes wrong, *he* did it'.

Once you have defined what you need, always ask yourself the question, 'Do I need to ask a professional outside organiser to help?' The professional organiser will probably have a wider knowledge of what there is on the market; what techniques are more applicable to

ACADEMIC, SCIENTIFIC, AND PROFESSIONAL...

... conferences, seminars, symposia, and meetings are our business. Exclusively. We plan them imaginatively. We organize them to the last detail. We manage them efficiently and economically. We also provide comprehensive back-up services — including the publication of proceedings. Telephone Peter Irving on 0223 323437 for all the details.

 **Conference Contact**
42 Devonshire Road Cambridge CB1 2BL
☎ 0223 323437 Telex: 81304 CBIOSC G Fax: 64317

---

your type of meeting; what hotels are more suitable for the meeting; where to hire (or buy) equipment; who can write the speeches (if necessary); where to contact guest speakers; what overseas sites would be suitable; what type of budget would be needed; how to narrow down or obtain a guest list; and what sort of invitation would work.

Whilst you would have to pay for this assistance, the knowledge and contacts a professional has can often help in obtaining discounts in certain areas. The cost involved must always be considered against the success you wish to achieve from the meeting.

I have already said that a properly run convention, or a conference, can be one of the most effective methods of communication. It is therefore important that it should be organised in the most effective manner; if this means that you need to pay for the assistance in order to organise it (or pay for the equipment or location, etc.) then do so. So many

Table 1.

Procedure		Breakdown	Important
Objectives	What for.	Who for. Where. When. Organisers. Meetings.	Send early notification to delegates.
Main features	Dates.	How long. Arrive/Depart. Venue rates. Provisional booking.	End the meeting before midday on Friday.
	Invitations.	VIPs. Guests. Exhibitors. Mailing list. Dates.	
	Agenda.	Timetable. Speakers. Handouts. Equipment. Publicity. Printer.	
	Finance.	Budget. Policy. Administrator. Credit arrangements.	
	Social activities.	Functions. Outing. Entertainment. Wives.	
Provisional programme	Timetable.	Rooms. When. Facilities. Transport. Personnel.	
	Speakers.	Booking. Equipment. Talk. Length. Fee. Transport.	
	Exhibits.	What. Exhibitor. Accommodation. Room space.	
	Confirmations.	Venue speaker. Entertainment. Speeches. Standbys.	

Venue bookings	Budget. Accommodation.	Rates. Extras. Menus. Protocol. Rooms. Dining. Functions. Exhibits. Parking.	Vary the menus. Check the cancellation list.
	Service.	Hospitality. Suites venue manpower. Contacts.	Have you considered the non-resident?
Timetable	Function.	When. Where. Who. Seating. Equipment. Manpower.	Avoid a tight schedule.
	Information.	Schedules. Seating plans. Organisers. Venue staff. Rates.	
Social activities	Functions.	Dinners. Speeches. Staffing. Equipment. Room plan.	
	Outing. Entertainment.	Transport. Babysitters. Times. Fee.	Choose entertainment to suit audience.
Joining instructions	Objectives. Place.	Accommodation. Residential/ non-residential	Despatch as soon as possible.
	Time. Timetable. Facilities.	Transport. Agenda. Meals.	Send venue brochures and local literature.

Table 1 – *cont.*

Procedure		Breakdown		Important
Equipment	Speakers. Functions. Exhibits.	What. When. Where. P.A. system. Floor plan. Room plan.	Power points. Light switches. Compatibility.	Can everyone see and hear? Do you need extension leads? Have spares ready. Leave time to set up equipment. Can the rooms be blacked out?
Catering	Morning coffee. Lunch. Afternoon tea. Evening meal.	When. Where. When. Type. Where. Pre-lunch drinks. When. Where. Style. Function or private.		Cater for dietary requirements. Appoint one man to control the bar. Observe protocol.
Check-back	Objectives. Timing. Communication. Information. Finance.	Functions. Deadlines. Duty rotas. Venue staff. Organisers. Complaint contact. Phone numbers. Delegates. Guests. Exhibitors. Mailing. Literature. Policy. Budget. Administration. Payments.		Get a 'crisis' contact.
Registration	Information. Personnel.	Spare literature and agendas. Signs. Badges. Administrators.		Has a message board been set up?

Welcome	Protocol.	VIPs. Honorarium. Welcome services.	
	Social.	Personnel.	
		Bar. Payment. Speech.	
Session checks	Functions.	Signs. Seating. Lighting. Heating. Ash trays. Water.	Handouts prepared?
	Equipment.	Working. Position. Plugged in. Volume. Lights. Scripts. Space.	
Security	Personnel. Documentation. Equipment. Materials.		
Emergencies	Spares. Briefing. Services.	Rooms. Equipment. Literature. Schedules. Duty rotas. Medical. Lost and found. Replacement. Insurance.	
	Back-up.	Personnel. Crisis contact.	
Conclusion	Equipment. Accounts.	Exhibits. Returned. Removed. Settled.	

Source: Meetings World (1969) Group Ltd.

companies (often through a lack of knowledge) spoil the event by trying to cut the costs. It is important to keep costs to acceptable limits and to work within budgets, but they do have to be realistic in relation to the results desired.

A word of warning! As well as the professional outside organiser, you will no doubt come across the amateur in-house expert. It is amazing how many people from the managing director to the sales director to the accountant suddenly become experts in set design, video production, speech writing, hotel choice, use of equipment, production or overseas travel. If you are selective in your choice of outside and inside help, your meeting will be successful. Be swamped by too many opinions and it will be a failure. The answer is to judge good advice from bad advice. Define the objective, determine your content, decide your method and enjoy yourself!

2 Budgeting for a conference

It has now been agreed; your company will have a conference in six months' time. And the task is squarely set on you. But before you allow your colleagues to disappear in a euphoric haze insist that you have one meeting of all personnel involved (and outside sources, such as your PR company, if they are involved) to discuss every item in detail. This is very important as you will need to have a clear understanding of exactly what is required before you can go away and prepare your budget. Organising a conference without a budget is just as bad, if not worse, than organising one without an objective and you cannot, *but cannot*, hide these expenses in the general overheads.

The budget that you create is a reflection of the overall perspective required of the company's future conference. How it is organised and what it tells the customers, public or workforce depends on its organisation, but what this organisation encompasses, in total, depends on the amount which the company can afford to spend. Naturally, you want the best possible venue, the most professional conference production, etc. for the prices. As different meetings require different venues, catering and preparation, so you must make absolutely sure that you, your sales or marketing director and whoever else is involved knows exactly what they would like and how much it is going to cost. It is no use after the event saying it cost too much and was not worth it – now is the time to decide not later.

Budgets are usually boring things and because of this, it is often difficult to pin people down for a direct answer. Some people tend to opt for the easiest path, which is simply to forget about the budget. But to follow this route is negligent and is liable to court disaster.

As there are many different types of conferences, meetings, seminars and conventions, we show all possible examples of expenditure, therefore some expenses noted may not be incurred by you. Only you know what your 'fixed costs' will be (insurance, transport, etc.) and what extras you need, these extras become your 'variable costs' (accommodation, entertainment, extra catering, badges, etc.). Should the company accountant look shocked at the end figure in your forecast, you can always attack the variables in order to reduce costs.

As a rule of thumb, place all indispensable items under the heading of fixed costs and those items which are nice, but not necessarily essential, place under the heading of variables. How do you tell which costs are variable and which are included in, say, the overall room hire charge? The safest thing to do is to list everything and then check with the different venue locations to see what facilities they offer and which are included in their package. Catering is a prime example. Hotels offer conference facilities that include a standard menu in their overall room hire rate (which also includes coffee, tea, etc.).

Additional services and equipment may be required and nowadays conference centres and hotels supply items such as different types of lighting, perhaps AV equipment, and possibly secretarial assistance. If the charges are not included in the room hire, you should

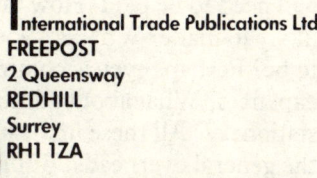

Conference Britain magazine is the leading journal for the UK based association and corporate exhibition, conference and incentive travel planner. Published by the ITP Meetings Division the world's largest publishing operation in the international meetings and exhibition industry with nearly forty years experience, Conference Britain has an enviable track record in today's fast moving UK industry.

It has established a reputation for keeping its readers abreast of the important trends, developments and events in the national and international exhibitions, conferences and incentive travel business. In each issue, news of the industry and its people, the latest products, prices, events, promotions, appointments, techniques and applications are fully reported. No other journal in this market rivals it for such complete coverage. What's more, it's FREE to organisers of events. Simply write to the ITP Meetings Division at the following address for full details.

International Trade Publications Ltd.
FREEPOST
2 Queensway
REDHILL
Surrey
RH1 1ZA

Or telephone Redhill (0737) 68611

ensure that they are competitive against quotes from outside contractors. You may be able to negotiate the room hire prices and any overnight accommodation booked. However, do make absolutely sure that you, and the venue locations' management (and later on the delegates) know who is paying for what.

The table opposite gives a list of all the possible expenses that may be incurred when planning a conference.

It would be useful here to reflect on some of the points found in Table 2. The first which merits our attention is the conference organiser's administrative costs. This is the precise area which needs close examination, and it is at this point that you may find that it becomes more cost-effective to hire a conference specialist to do the organising for you.

There is no precise way to arrive at the cost which you and the extra administrative expenditure will make to the overall cost of the conference. Perhaps the simplest method is to work out how much time you expect to take in order to complete your routine tasks, and whether or not you need assistance from any other source. Ask your accounts department for your hourly rate, and then add on the National Insurance rate. Work out what other tasks you were supposed to do during this time but because of the increased workload either someone else will have to do them or overtime will need to be paid. How many telephone calls are you likely to make? What are your travel expenses likely to be? Perhaps even accommodation and entertainment expenses? What about additional postage and stationery? All these items usually disappear into the general overheads. But the company should know what a conference costs to organise, so work out separately what each item will cost, including your time. When comparing costs to the conference organiser's quotation, remember that the organiser may be able to get discounts which you would not – but do ask. The example on page 23 lists expenses likely to be incurred, giving rough sample costings.

2 BUDGETING FOR A CONFERENCE

Table 2. The budget

Venue (basic cost)
Speakers' fees
   travelling/accommodation expenses
PR costs (extra publicity)
   admin. time, press releases
Marketing costs
   admin. costs, advertisement, brochure, extra letterheads and envelopes, mailing
Special conference printing
   badges, conference reports, invitations, programmes, special sign posts, maps
AV equipment
   autocue, slides, speakers, sound equipment, teleprompter, video and/or sound tapes, video equipment
Lighting
Microphones
Extra services
   extra furniture, secretarial, telephone, telex, translation, other
Stage set, flowers
Transport
   air, rail, road
Catering
   coffees/teas/refreshments, entertainment, functions, pre/post conference meal
Accommodation
Insurance
Rehearsal costs
Overdraft
Conference organiser and admin. costs
   SUB TOTAL

Percentage for inflation	5 per cent
Percentage for increase in expenditure	5/10 per cent
VAT	15 per cent
TOTAL	

EXAMPLE
Salaried employee on £12,000 per annum = £6.24 per hour.

Average time to organise an inter-company conference including travelling time to venue, say 100 hours = £624 + £65.21 (N.I.) = £689.21

	£	
Lost time 100 hours	689.21	
Conference time	689.21	
Assistant's time	340.00	
Travelling expenses	62.00	
Telephone	35.00	(including VAT)
Misc. expenses	125.00	(including (VAT)
Increased postage	6.80	
Extra stationery	15.00	
Total	1,962.22	

And this is just a minimum and does not include any direct conference costs. If large or more specialised meetings are organised, or if you are paid more than the initial sum in the example, then the cost increases or decreases depending on your salary.

Those often forgotten costs

Leaving VAT off your budget forecast is a common enough error but other hidden costs also need to be taken into account, for example, inflation, overdraft charges on fixed costs (assuming your business like many others has an overdraft), unforeseen expenses.

Let us take the first of these, inflation. At the time of writing, inflation is low but who is to say when it will increase again, after all it has a somewhat mercurial temperament and its rise and fall depends upon many influencing factors. Some conferences are organised a year ahead of time (even two years) and what happens on the inflation front is therefore very important. Although average company conferences are planned some four to six months ahead, inflation

2 BUDGETING FOR A CONFERENCE

still needs to be considered and entered in. Even with the current rate of inflation, assuming your conference is planned six months ahead, overall costs will have shown an increase of 2.7 per cent. Suppose your fixed costs are, say, £7,000, then inflation could add £189 to your final bill!

Most businesses run on an overdraft. Your firm might be lucky and only have, say, 1 per cent or 2 per cent over base rate. This means that the company will be charged 12 per cent to 13 per cent (maybe more) on any conference costs incurred while the account is in the 'red'. Then there is VAT at 15 per cent. Despite the fact that you can reclaim VAT (if you are registered) the company will still have to pay it out first.

Unforeseen expenses can create a noticeable gap in your budget. Anything can cause this increase, from the chairman inviting along special clients on an all-expenses paid trip, to your salesforce ordering rounds of drinks before and after the conference and putting them on the company's conference bill. (Or, if organising a meeting abroad, the currency fluctuation can dramatically increase your bill.) You might be lucky – it might only be a few extra telephone calls – but no matter how carefully you plan, unforeseen expenses will occur. The simple answer is to allow yourself an extra amount, say, 5 per cent to 8 per cent on top of your total budget amount, plus VAT, of course.

Quotations
As your planning progresses, you will require quotations from many different sources. Ask for firm costs, which should be possible if the time scale is not too distant. Three quotations per service are usually asked for (in writing). Before making a decision re-read these quotations to see that they allow for all the items originally asked for, and all the items that you feel you need.

After deciding on each service, reply in writing, re-affirming the price quoted and whether or not it includes VAT. Also confirm if the cost will be over a fixed time period or not. Keep all the correspondence in a special *Budget* file, for future reference.

Cash flow forecast

Now that you have got your forecast agreed with your managing director, and doubtless with the company accountant or bookkeeper, they will want to know the time scale for all these extra payments; will the items in month one cost £500 while those in month two cost only £250? The accountant will need to know this as the extra cash requirement will influence the business accounts balance: therefore a cash flow forecast becomes necessary. This need not be an elaborate plan but one which shows, on a monthly basis, when payments are likely to fall due. If your conference is to be held in six months' time, then the bill for the venue will become due in the seventh month. On the other hand, expenses incurred by you visiting the venue site will probably need paying in month two; the invoice for special brochures and badges may need paying in month five or month six. Table 3 shows you what to do.

Table 3. Cash flow forecast

Items	Month 1	Month 2	Month 3	Month 4	Month 5	Month 6
	£	£	£	£	£	£
Admin. costs		30		30	40.45	60.00
Hire of projector						140.00
Hotel accommodation		25				40.25
Entertainment						65.00
Conference room						165.00
Extra catering						125.00
Printing				20.60		135.00
Misc.		10.80		12.50	16.00	
VAT		5.37		4.97	2.40	100.54
Total		71.17		68.07	58.85	830.79

2 BUDGETING FOR A CONFERENCE

But how do you keep tabs on what the expense has been in each month? The simplest way is to keep your own monthly sheet of expenses and enter in each invoice as it comes in (see Table 4). You should organise for all conference invoices to be sent to you first. Check each one against the quotation received and if correct, enter who the invoice is from, date received, amount, sub-total, VAT and total. If there is any discrepancy due to unsatisfactory standard of goods, or the figure does not agree with the quotation, query the invoice in writing to the supplier within seven working days of receiving it – and hold on to the invoice until you receive a satisfactory answer.

Table 4.   Monthly bought ledger sheet

Month: 3 (July)

Date	Invoice no.	Sub-total £	VAT £	Total £
7.9.'86	K200 PZ	200.00	30.00	230.00
12.10.'86	00697	165.00	24.75	189.75
14.11.'86	001829	35.00	5.25	40.25
Monthly total £		400.00	60.00	460.00

If your conference is a very large one, there may be many items in the same category. It will be worth your while to set up an additional system whereby each category of expenses has its own sheet and each invoice is marked up showing who it is from, date, invoice number, amount, VAT, and total. Note whether it was passed for payment, a tick alongside each entry will suffice.

Higher standards of print, higher standards of service for print buyers

Whether your require a full colour brochure, news-sheets, packaging or mailpacks, Errey's puts high priority on giving you the best quality print.

But there's something the Errey's Printers Group believes is just as important — and that's **service**.

We can work closely with you to agree the most appropriate and **cost-saving** methods of production.

You'll also find we can tailor a service to your particular requirements — whatever they may be! For example, Errey's has built a reputation for consistently achieving very short lead times.

You won't be kept waiting for your print either. Errey's offers you daily van deliveries and collections throughout London and the South East, and there's a complimentary Central London messenger service. **The next step is simple!**

Look into Errey's standards of service for yourself. Call Maurice Fisher on Heathfield ☎ **(04352) 6211**, and ask for an estimate on your next print job. Or ask us to visit you with a range of our recent work. If there's any kind of print you'd particularly like to see, simply let us know.

You'll appreciate the difference

Errey's
Printers Group

Errey's Printers Group, Streatfield Road, Heathfield, East Sussex TN21 8HX

Table 5.   Itemised sheet

Category: Printing

Date	Suppliers name	Invoice no.	Sub-total	VAT	Total
			£	£	£
10.10.'86	Kwik Printers	K200PZ	200.00	30.00	230.00
12.11.86	Namecall Ltd	86126	63.70	9.56	73.26
Total			263.70	39.56	303.26

After entering each invoice on your sheet, initial it or mark it 'cleared for payment' before passing it on to your accounts department. You may want to keep a photocopy on file in case a particular supplier is sending in part orders which will need checking through to ensure that items have not been duplicated.

Conference organising should always be done in as

2 BUDGETING FOR A CONFERENCE

business-like manner as possible. None more so than in the budgeting of conference accounts. Once a system has been put in order then it is far easier to keep, easier to use, and errors and frayed tempers are subsequently reduced.

Drop Anchor at the
ALBERT DOCK
Conference and Exhibition Centre

Looking for a venue that's convenient, efficient and just a bit different?

You'll find it at Britain's largest group of Grade 1 listed buildings, The Albert Dock. A versatile complex offering facilities for conferences and exhibitions of all sizes including large halls & seminar rooms.

All this plus problem-free parking, invigorating sea-air and the effective, professional back-up services you need to ensure a successful event.

For further information, contact Alan Silver, Commercial Manager, on 051-709 7373.

· THE ALBERT DOCK ·
· L I V E R P O O L ·

Photograph: KEVIN CUMMINS

3 The programme

The decision has been made, budgets have been agreed and you know what you want to achieve. Now you need to arrange the agenda and contact prospective speakers, obviously keeping in mind any theme you wish to run through your conference. You also need to decide who your audience is and how to invite them.

The audience, contents and theme have to be borne in mind as interlocking pieces of your objective. If the content and theme is incompatible with your audience, then you will not gain its interest and will fail to achieve your objective. It is all too easy to get carried away with the euphoria of arranging a meeting which is self-indulgent in its content and style because the organiser likes the way it is done without reference to the type of people in the audience. You would not get a troupe of topless dancers to put over a message to an audience of nuns, would you? That may be a little extreme, but it is the sort of thing that could happen. So consider carefully who your audience will be.

If you know the audience, so much the better. You will know what programme you can organise and also how, to a great extent, it will react to it. In this case,

3 THE PROGRAMME

you probably know what you can get away with and what will help get the message across.

If the audience is unknown, you may need to make some assumptions about what would be acceptable in the programme. If your audience are city bankers or top level investment experts, you will normally need a different approach than if they were Australian sheep farmers! I am not saying that your objective should change – just that the means to achieve the objective may vary.

The other advantage of knowing your audience (either through direct employment or by association or trade links) is it makes the invitation that much easier to design, and also makes it easier to approach your prospective delegates. Always bear in mind, of course, that they may still need some form of incentive in order to be persuaded to attend the meeting. If last year's meeting was a disaster, or they were unclear what the meeting was about, you may still have problems in getting them to attend.

If you do not know your audience, the problem may be slightly wider because you will need to find the people to invite. You may have a list of invitees through your company or association, but you may also need to get your message across to people who perhaps do not know of your company's existence yet. At the moment you may not be aware of theirs either!

If the latter is the case, there are many reputable direct mail firms or list brokers who can help. They will help to define your market area and list of invitees. Obviously, there may be other trade associations willing to supply the names and addresses of their members. Most 'professions' or 'trades' have some form of association membership these days and, subject to the message you want to put across, may be only too willing to help – albeit for a fee. You will find, however, that some of them are extremely loathe to release a list of members – so beware as this avenue may not be open to you.

Reference was made earlier to the invitation of known people, and the need to have an incentive to attract them to attend. Obviously this applies to all invitees. By incentive, I do not necessarily mean a draw for a holiday or a bottle of wine (although 'tangible' incentives can help), but the incentive to attend the meeting because the message sounds attractive and worthwhile. Participants need to feel that time at a conference or presentation will be well spent and beneficial to them. You have to create, by the invitation, a desire to go to the meeting. You need to excite them enough to attend, but at the same time not give too much of the content away.

The name of your company or even the subject matter itself, will be, in some cases, quite a draw. If you feel it is not enough, what else can be done? Some companies have offered a weekend in Rome, or a trip round the world as a way of getting people to attend. The names of all attendees go into a hat, and the prize draw is made at the end of the meeting. This method can work well, although it does not always have the desired effect. You have to judge how your prospective audience will react. No matter how good the incentive, you still have to get your message across once the attendees are there, so do not confuse one with the other. In the context of the programme itself, the use of guest speakers is discussed a little later in the chapter. Such a guest speaker could possibly be an attraction for people to attend the meeting, and if so, perhaps you should consider mentioning the person by name on your invitation. If you are paying a celebrity to participate in your meeting, use that person not only in the meeting itself but also as an attraction for people to come along. Note, however, that you will probably need the celebrity's permission to do so, and he will also need to know what will be printed on the invitation.

One other point on invitations, how many of them need to be sent out in order to get the number of people you want in the audience? Once again, it depends on whether the audience is 'in-house' or 'external'. The 'in-house' invitees will obviously respond better (unless you really do have a bad name

3 THE PROGRAMME

with the staff!), so it is the response of the unknown invitees which is much more difficult to judge. There are many factors such as, are you known? Have you a guest speaker? If so, who? Is the subject matter alone a big enough incentive? Are your competitors running meetings at the same time? (This is an important thing to check if you can but it is often overlooked – especially important for a press launch.) Are you offering a draw prize? Is the venue attractive? (The venue can be a great incentive to attend – more about that in Chapter 4.)

Naturally, the above factors can affect numbers but as a rough rule of thumb, if you want 100 people to attend the meeting (and you and they have not 'met' before), invite approximately 800–900 people, possibly 1,000. The likelihood is that 120 to 150 people will accept and of these something in the region of 100 will turn up (there is always a drop-out factor). These situations vary from one event to another.

So what about the programme? How are you going to make it interesting and informative and achieve your objective? As mentioned earlier, the range of meetings is extremely wide and objectives equally so. For the sake of argument, therefore, let us assume that the objective is to run a three day meeting in the UK for your top sales people (and their partners) to recognise their achievements and discuss company policy for the coming year. On the last day they will be joined by the balance of the sales force and attend a new product's presentation. (This assumes that venue and budget have already been agreed; the ideas given only deal with the programme and the possibilities open to you.)

Allow them adequate travelling time at either end of the meeting. Let us assume that the conference runs from noon on Monday to 4 pm on Wednesday, with the last contingent arriving at about 11 am on the Wednesday.

The conference lasts for three days, and during that time you have to mix up reward, recognition, a sales meeting, some motivation and a product launch – and you have got delegates' partners as well! The right balance needs to be struck on the first two days between work and play. You need to run some business meetings obviously, but you also need to give the attendees some relaxation, either organised or not.

Do you need a guest speaker? If so, is that person purely a chairman for the business meeting or a speaker on a specific subject? Or do you need both? Does he or she need to be there for all three days or just for the last day? Celebrities can provide two important factors for meetings. They create for your company a professional image (if you are prepared to pay for a celebrity, you are obviously taking both the subject and the audience very seriously), and they help to make the meeting run a lot more smoothly by lending their expertise and experience to the procedures. For a three day meeting, I would suggest that a celebrity would be best used by coming in on the second day in order to get involved in some form of fun or relaxation (more of that shortly), speak at a dinner in the evening and chair the product launch on the following day. As a bit of fun, and if it is possible, why not have the celebrity arrive at lunchtime by balloon or helicopter!

Other conference content

But what about the other content and the other speakers? You need a couple of business sessions in the first two days to deal with the recognition and company approach in the future. Because the attendees are the top people in your salesforce, they will expect (and rightly) to meet the top management in the company (if the company does not feel the same way, it has probably got some problems). You would probably need, therefore, the managing director and the sales director to talk and to supplement this with one or two other important executives. Other executives would also need to be there, as well as this top echelon, in order to host the guests during the two days.

Over the two days, I would suggest a business

"...The best known and known by the Best!"

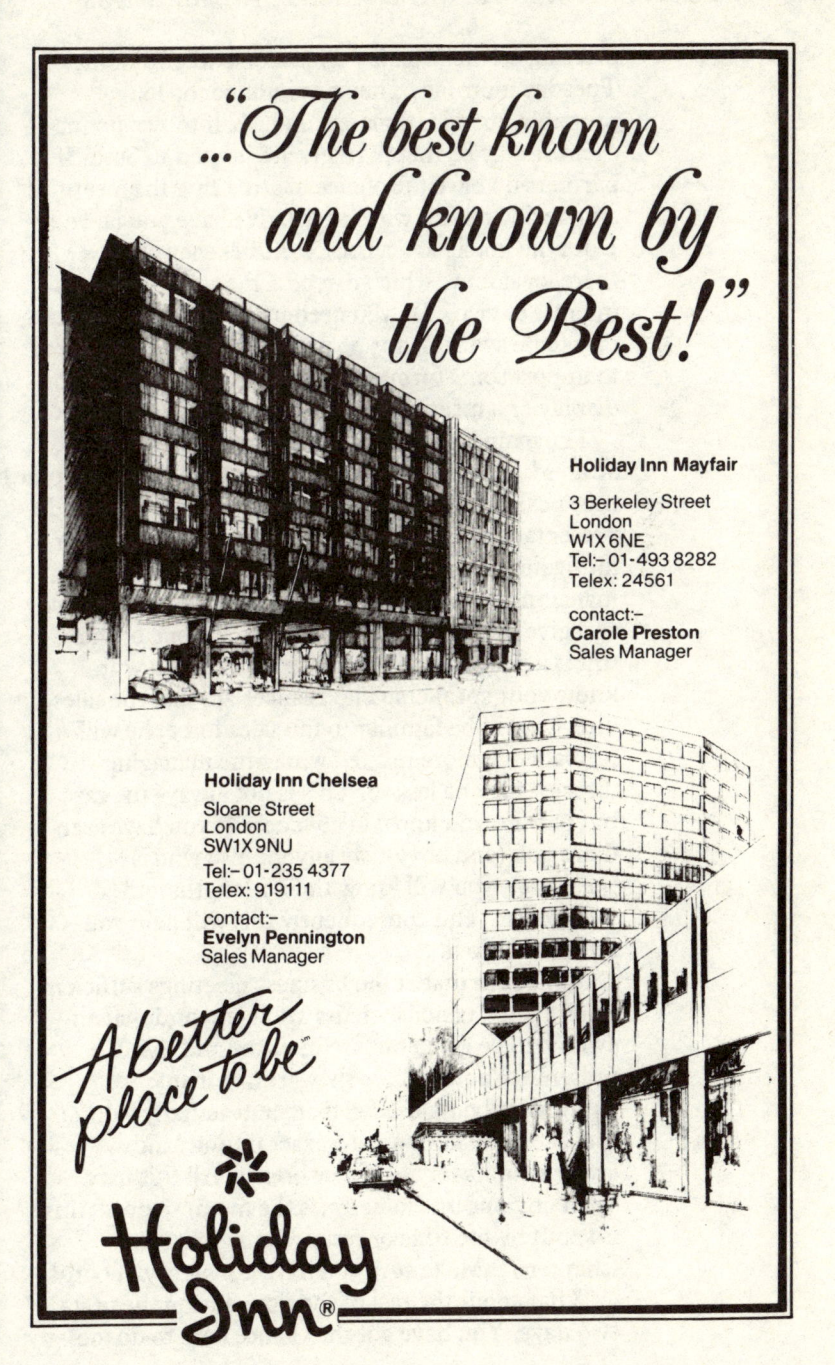

Holiday Inn Mayfair

3 Berkeley Street
London
W1X 6NE
Tel:- 01-493 8282
Telex: 24561

contact:-
Carole Preston
Sales Manager

Holiday Inn Chelsea

Sloane Street
London
SW1X 9NU

Tel:- 01-235 4377
Telex: 919111

contact:-
Evelyn Pennington
Sales Manager

A better place to be

Holiday Inn®

meeting on the Monday afternoon and one on the Tuesday morning. They need not be too long, probably no more than one and a half to two hours each. It may be that partners are invited to both. If partners do have the choice of attending the meetings and decide not to, what alternative have you laid on? Does the hotel have leisure facilities they can use? Are there local tours which can be arranged or places of interest to visit? Do you need to arrange for coaches or cars to be available for people to go out? Do you need to import some form of alternative, such as a fashion display or a meeting of their own?

The main business meetings themselves should always be well prepared and (bearing in mind Chapter 1) use speakers, support slides, different speakers and presentations. You have got the top sales people so motivate them as well as inform them. The managing director may want to chair both meetings and give the main company address at one of them – this is a good idea. For these meetings you will know your speakers. The chances are that the sales director will be familiar to the sales force; he will probably be more relaxed whilst the managing director may be less so. This is not always the case but how do you know in advance? If you have seen them talk (and obviously anyone else who is speaking), you will know their strengths and weaknesses, and consequently this will help you know what to do.

Make sure that at the business meetings sufficient water, pads, pencils, chairs are there, and that any awards to be given out are in place (and the presenter knows where they are); that any equipment being used is there and actually works; that the hotel knows your exact timings and arrangements for coffees or breaks. All this may seem obvious but sometimes the intent to do all this is spoilt by the time or resources to do it (see Chapter 7). Make sure you have got plenty of both!

What about the rest of the time during the first two days. You have got the chance here to do too

3 THE PROGRAMME

much or do nothing. Somewhere in between is the happy medium. Dependent upon the hotel (and I am assuming that you have chosen the right one!) and the time of the year, you could put together a few 'special' events. You could arrange for a 'superstar' type competition over the two days (or one afternoon) including clay pigeon shooting, tennis, croquet, swimming, bridge or snooker. All the events should not be too serious, and some of them could be amusing events, such as three-legged races. These can be a lot of fun especially if you can get the managing director and the celebrity to join in. (Do not forget, if arranging outdoor activities, the English weather may necessitate some indoor contingency plans!)

But the economic pressures of recent years have resulted in the tendency to pack as much business content into the meetings. Despite this development, there remains the need for 'social periods' within overall programmes. When you arrange the meals, think of different things to do. If there is a speciality restaurant nearby, go out on the Monday evening or for Tuesday lunch. (If you can, have one or two meals outside the hotel.) Arrange a welcome coffee break, cocktails or buffet lunch on the Monday. There may be people you have not met so let them mingle and get to know each other. Why not a champagne breakfast and a jazz band on the Tuesday? Weather permitting, why not breakfast or lunch by the pool side? You could even surprise your guests at dinner one night by having the band appear from one of the rooms halfway through the meal – this would change an apparently ordinary meal to one that certainly becomes a 'fun' party and gets the conference off to a great start. Does the hotel arrange theme evenings (cockney sing-a-longs, medieval banquets, Roman toga parties, etc.)? If they do, why not arrange one of these. Some people are a bit wary of theme parties, especially if it means people dressing up, but many companies have run them successfully and they can be tremendous entertainment.

You should also lay on a really good 'convention dinner' (banquet) for your guests, probably on the Tuesday night (see Chapter 8 on conference catering). Use the celebrity to make a witty after-dinner speech. Perhaps you need to bring in a cabaret or a comedian, a band or disco for dancing. And give everybody a small suitable gift.

Whatever you do over the two days, try and get some fun, some participation, and some involvement within the group.

On the Wednesday, your business meeting for the product launch is again a key element of the whole conference. It has got to maintain the excellence in the top producers' minds, which they have enjoyed over the first two days. Make sure that all the sales people, including the top producers and those joining for the day, know how professional the company is and why they should be proud of being part of it. The new product has got to be presented to everyone if the company wants them to sell it.

Use the celebrity to chair the meeting and give a small welcome and warm up talk. Get the managing director to follow with perhaps an overview of why the company is launching the new product. What are the market forces at that time that makes it necessary. You will then need a couple of speeches to explain exactly what the product is, how it works and why it is better than your competitor's brand. Depending on the product, show it either on film or actually have one there. Use proper presentation techniques, such as audio visual or video, to make the meeting professional. This is probably an area where a professional outside organiser can help – he will know what you can or cannot do and whether it would lend itself to the type of presentation you wish to make. Chapter 5 gives details of the different types of presentation equipment.

After the presentation, give everybody a good lunch. This may be either a buffet or a sit-down

3 THE PROGRAMME

depending upon your numbers. Whatever you do, why not give it a bit of extra flair by decorating the room with coloured banners or coloured balloons. Use coasters or give away pens to brighten things up. Bring on the jazz band again. Give everybody a pack about the company and its product. It is important that people finish up on a memorable note at such a conference.

There are many different forms of meetings, the above is merely a possible requirement. It may be that the meeting you are arranging is only a part of the above, but bear in mind the comments and suggestions. Whatever the meeting and whatever you decide to do, plan it properly, make sure you have the right ingredients for work and play, and above all, rehearse the programme properly.

Conference Bureau

have pleasure in inviting

All Conference Organisers

....

to use their FREE COMPUTERISED VENUE FINDING SERVICES FOR ALL YOUR EVENTS...

ANY TIME, ANY SIZE, ANYWHERE.

RSVP to: Caroline J. Connabeer or Denise Ellis

Their 20 years experience in business and hotels ensures a personalised and professional service

Conference Bureau Ltd, Holberg House, 33 Lewes Way, Croxley Green, Rickmansworth, Hertfordshire. WD3 3SW
Tel: 0923 48527

4 The importance of selecting a suitable venue

Over the past ten years there have been more changes in terms of content, purpose and requirements of conference organising than throughout the previous three decades. The major influencing factor has undoubtedly been the economic climate. Companies have had to become more competitive in their approach to outside influences; the ability of the workforce to translate the company's ideas and products has also taken on a significant purpose. Conferences are now expected to be more meaningful and productive – it goes without saying that this new status demands that conference expenditure produces worthwhile results.

Until the middle of the 1970s, typical sales conferences would be held in a leisure resort, and spouses would have been invited. These gatherings would last from one weekend to the next, with only a few hours spent on business sessions. Of the four days, only one day might be taken up with speeches of welcome, presentation of long service awards or top sales staff of the year awards: the rest of the time would be devoted to sea, sun and sports – all at the company's expense. Nowadays such events are

Brocket Hall

England's Finest Incentive & Conference Venue

Brocket Hall, the home of Lord and Lady Brocket, is situated 35 minutes' North of London's Park Lane. Set in over 1,000 acres of beautiful parkland, with a 6,000 ft private airport on the perimeter of the estate, Brocket Hall is England's most exclusive residential conference and incentive venue. The Hall, with 46 luxurious double bedrooms, provides every modern facility. It is the only stately home which offers these facilities on an exclusive basis to its clients be it either for a magnificent dinner party or week-long conference, incentive or private event.
Brocket Hall is available all year round and regularly hosts political and corporate meetings and provides unique surroundings of unparalleled style, service and privacy.

Brocket Hall · Welwyn · Hertfordshire · AL8 7XG
Tel: Welwyn Garden (0707) 335241   Telex 893005

Find the right conference venue and the chances are you've found yourself a successful conference.

Anyone can choose a location that has all the right facilities, finding one with the right atmosphere is a lot harder.

That's where Meeting Point comes in.

We understand that no two conferences are ever the same. A small meeting may want intimate surroundings whilst a large sa conference may need a more formal setting

Using the latest computer technology staff will first select from over 200 of the fin hotel and conference venues, a shortlist possible locations.

Then, using our unrivalled knowlec we will help you choose the one that rea suits the style of your conference

> Given 60 seconds could you say which of these conference venues is right for your next conference? We could.
>
> Meeting Point
>
> Ring 01-567 3444

Checking availability and booking con...nation can be done immediately.

But the personal touch doesn't end ...re. On arrival you will be met by a Meeting ...nt Manager supported by his specially ...ned staff.

They will help you make the best of our ...ssive investment in new equipment and ...ure everything runs smoothly from the welcoming drinks to the closing speeches.

It all adds up to a service that's fast, efficient and above all run by people who really understand how to make your conference successful.

We're waiting for your call.

Trusthouse Forte Hotels

At least they agreed on how to get there.

British Airways have more flights to London from more places around the world than any other airline.

That's why most delegates vote for us to fly them to their conference.

For further information please contact your British Airways appointed travel agent, or British Airways Travel Services Office, Comet House, P.O. Box 10, Hounslow, Middx. TW6 2JA, telephone 01-750 5776. Or contact British Airways sales office.

BRITISH AIRWAYS
The world's favourite airline.

4 THE IMPORTANCE OF SELECTING A SUITABLE VENUE

marked with a much greater degree of austerity, with business discussion the order of the day.

As a result of this change, the location of a venue is now more likely to be chosen for its geographical and logistical convenience, rather than from the entertainment aspect, while the conference itself will involve only personnel to whom the relevant conference information needs to be imparted. Awards will be made during dinner so as not to curtail valuable discussion time.

Organising a successful conference or meeting is a combination of many different facets, and none more important than selecting a suitable venue site. It is a sad reflection that consideration as to suitable venue sites, so crucial to a function, is frequently left to executives who, although no doubt capable within their day-to-day responsibilities, are not equipped to make a decision which can influence, to a large degree, the success or failure of a conference. In this chapter we make a number of observations about the structure and demands made on the company and its organiser when setting up a conference or meeting. These pointers should reflect the conference needs when selecting ultimate venues.

First let us define what we mean by 'venue'. When deciding on a suitable location to hold your meeting, there is a tendency to think only in terms of hotels as the ideal location, and possibly some of the purpose-built conference centres which have been developed in recent years. Instead, product launches (or what is increasingly being termed 'Industrial Theatre') could use certain exhibition centres, cinemas, or indeed buildings which house theatrical performances. In another instance, although room hire costs and banqueting are of prime consideration, the eventual selection of the venue site may be influenced by the need for an academic environment, such as those facilities and services now provided by universities and colleges. Although the availability of both universities and colleges can be restricted to out of term periods and to weekends, these alternative venue sites have made a substantial in-road into the corporate meetings' sector. Company and association conferences are now an important source of revenue to both universities and colleges alike. To find out more, contact the administrative department of your local university or college.

Some conferences last a maximum of three days, depending upon their purpose. The participants are expected to return to their jobs the morning after the final session, or just as early as transportation arrangements permit. At this length of conference, there are now few companies that allow accompanying spouses but, of course, this will depend on the purpose and objective of your conference. For one day conferences, the pre-conference instructions given out by the organiser frequently state, 'in order to avoid unnecessary additional nights' accommodation, where practical, you should arrive for the opening at 09.00 hours on Monday, and depart after the last business session at 18.00 hours'. Time and expenditure are both carefully considered.

Although indications of humorous episodes seep through, as they frequently do on these occasions, the underlying fact is that the conference of today, unlike its predecessors, has a significant and unmistakable purpose. This is not altogether surprising when one calculates the cost of travel and accommodation, together with other expenses, and add to that the time employees have to spend away from their jobs.

The programme for a typical one day meeting is dictated by the time period involved and the type of meeting planned. If the meeting is crammed into one day allowing little time for delays or extended sessions, consider the possibility of stretching it across a two-day period – if the content is highly technical, then this in itself could necessitate extending the conference. This is, of course, applicable to conferences where all the delegates will be together in one hall. But what happens if the conference or meeting is, say, of a more academic nature?

Over two or three days, conference time can be

4 THE IMPORTANCE OF SELECTING A SUITABLE VENUE

devoted to syndicate sessions. The employees or delegates can be split up into groups of five or six and given a series of specific case studies to resolve. During the afternoon of the last day, each group leader presents the conclusions to the plenary session of the conference.

Understanding your needs

How do you select a suitable venue site? The first thing to do is to consider the needs of the conference or meeting, and its purpose. This would appear to be stating the obvious, but although acknowledging the dearth of purpose-built conference facilities (many hotels, for example, have ballrooms which are conveniently labelled 'conference rooms') far too often companies choose a location without considering the content and requirements of the forthcoming conference. So ask yourself the following questions.

1. How long will the programme be?
2. How many speakers are there?
3. How far will the delegates and speakers have to travel? (Take the furthest distance from the proposed location.)
4. What is the expenditure?
5. What are the conference aims?
6. How far from the office (or head office) should the meeting be held?
7. How many delegates or guests will need accommodation?

The answers to these questions will give you an idea of the 'ideal' venue site. The question of the location can then be looked at more closely.

What to look for when selecting a venue

Have you decided to have your meeting close to your head office or equidistant between all your offices? Check travel times and see which would be the most appropriate. But do try not to select a site that is too remote – it might be equidistant but the extra time spent trying to find it may mean your conference getting off to a late start.

International Students House

Business Functions Conferences, Seminars

International Students House is the ideal conference centre for organisations seeking excellent facilities for up to 300 guests at an economic cost in Central London.

Our professional Conference Team, our superb catering and convenient location in one of London's most beautiful buildings overlooking Regents Park, have enabled us to build a reputation that is the envy of our competitors.

Why not make an appointment to see for yourself?

For full details either phone
Alison Hardy, Conference Manager,
on 01-631 3223 or write to:
INTERNATIONAL STUDENTS HOUSE,
229 Great Portland Street, London W1N 5DH.

4 THE IMPORTANCE OF SELECTING A SUITABLE VENUE

In areas where hotels and other venues enjoy high occupancy, your company may have a restricted choice. In order to overcome this, you first need to compile a list of suitable venues and carefully check availability of your chosen dates. Remember to ask whether adequate room accommodation is available.

Where the company conference is devoted entirely to business, checking on suitable entertainment does not present a problem, but should spouses accompany participants, then there are a number of questions which need to be asked. What are the sports facilities like? Are shops close to the hotel or in the hotel? Are there any sites of interest to visit? If so, what transport arrangements are there? There are two books which will help in finding out information. *The Conference Green Book* and *The Conference Blue Book*. Both titles are published by Spectrum Communications Group (01-749 3061).

The site visit

Once your list of possible venue sites has been narrowed down, the time has come to pay each one a visit. Check that the rooms are the right size and what facilities are included in the price.

The next step is to identify an executive at each site who has a track record of handling corporate events. The person must be able to respond to your conference needs but, equally important, the person has to be in a position to give advice on the logistics of your programme relating to the site. There is a myth about the role of venue sales people in this respect. They are there to sell the venue to you and, unless the person doubles up in another relevant capacity, to all intents and purposes once it has been sold to you, their job is over. Ask for either the banqueting or conference executives, they are the people who are normally responsible for managing events on site. And they should be able to state clearly what can and what cannot be done. Do not be afraid to ask them what other conferences or meetings have been held there, then references can be taken up.

What size of room do you think you will need? Of course, this depends entirely on the number of attendees and the type of meeting – conference, seminar, workshop or presentation. Allow adequate space for seating and movement, a guide to space requirements is given in Chapter 5. If planning a workshop then allow extra space for tables and other furnishings.

Check on the room's ventilation to see if it is adequate, if not, then you may have a problem. It is difficult to state whether smoking should or should not be allowed, but take into consideration that a room becomes stuffy when smoking is permitted. If ceilings are low then the air becomes smoke-filled quickly. This can be very discomforting for other participants. You have three options. First, allow smoking in the room. Second, disallow smoking but allow for adequate breaks in the programme as some people cannot go too long without lighting up a cigarette. Third, section the room so that smokers can be seated on either the left or the right-hand side, whichever is nearest to the windows or ventilation point.

When selecting a suitable venue site, you need to consider whether an ante room will be necessary, for example, delegates may wish to talk to the company's management. If the room is needed, can the site accommodate this requirement? – it should be adjoining the meeting room.

What about hotel accommodation? Are there enough rooms available either on the conference site or close by? Should the overnight accommodation be at a separate location, then visit the hotel to find out what the state of the accommodation is like.

Will the venue site allow for the reception area and conference room to be decorated with banners, posters, etc.? If so, discuss with the conference manager the best positions.

What about parking arrangements? Are they close at hand and can they be reserved for the conference?

Will you need secretarial help? Again, ask the venue site if they can provide this. What about telephones

4 THE IMPORTANCE OF SELECTING A SUITABLE VENUE

and other forms of communication? Whatever you do, a telephone should not be put into a conference room otherwise you will be asking for frequent interruptions.

Selecting a suitable venue is of paramount importance. However, there are probably more errors made in this area than in any other because all the factors which can make a difference between a successful event or otherwise have not been thought through.

Some meetings are scheduled at short notice and as a result it can become necessary to accept whatever is available. The common error when making this important decision is simple – the organiser has not established beforehand the criteria before considering the requirements for the event. Such errors can be costly too, not only in financial terms, but also the reduced input by the delegates because the venue does not lend itself to the objectives of the meeting. For example, the early start to an event could mean that delegates will need to arrive the evening before, and that necessitates additional expenditure in the form of meals and accommodation. A similar situation can apply, of course, if an event closes too late for the participants to return to their homes. It appears all very basic, and yet there are so many instances where this was not considered until it was too late to change the programme. But not only the timing of appearances needs to be considered, seating and banqueting is another. Also noise levels create a problem, for example, air conditioning and heating systems can produce distracting droning noises. They need to be checked.

Competition from other events can adversely affect your function. So find out from the site if any other events are taking place, and precisely what they are. A classic example of a very bad choice of location happened when a company found itself competing with a musical rehearsal, which was taking place in an adjacent room. The noise was such that the training session was interrupted a number of times. One could blame the venue management for such a conflict of interest because they should have checked the two bookings to find whether they were compatible. However, this was no consolation in this instance, and the company concerned took their organising executive to task for the error – and the directors vented their anger by dismissing the unfortunate executive.

There are other noise factors which can be equally distracting, such as road works, the maintenance of lifts, adjacent refurbishing or quite simply, raised voices. All these things can spoil a presentation and compete for the delegates' attention.

But such things need not happen if basic research is conducted at the outset. Once you are satisfied that the facilities you have seen can contribute and not detract from the event, then and only then have you found a suitable site.

Only after checking and double-checking all possible requirements, services, costs and locations, should you decide on a final venue site. This final decision may require a second site visit. And remember to confirm in writing all arrangements and understandings. If room numbers for accommodation have not yet been finalised, state a specific time when exact figures will be given and ask the hotel to tentatively reserve 'xx' number of rooms.

So far we have not discussed potential problems. If there has to be one common problem encountered by companies it must be the failure of many conference facilities to provide adequate sound systems. Obviously in a small room with a limited number of participants in, say, a training session, the difficulty should not arise. However, the majority of rooms which accommodate larger numbers of delegates will need the additional installation of a sound reinforcement system. This can be the case in even the most modern hotels because their existing in-house microphones and loud speaker equipment is simply not powerful enough. Hoteliers are most reluctant to admit this, but the fact remains that conferences have

4 THE IMPORTANCE OF SELECTING A SUITABLE VENUE

Interlingua TTI
THE COMPLETE LANGUAGE SERVICE

PLANNING AN INTERNATIONAL CONFERENCE?
Let Interlingua TTI handle the languages!

INTERPRETERS: Simultaneous, consecutive & ad-hoc for all occasions.

EQUIPMENT: Sophisticated simultaneous packages tailored to your conference requirements or portable equipment for liaison interpreting.

SUPPORT SERVICES: Translation of documents, typesetting and print. Multi-lingual hostesses and recording/transcription facilities available.

Also – Audioconferencing – interpreting over the 'phone! All languages handled professionally in any location worldwide.

Call our interpreting division on 01-240 5361 **Interlingua TTI Ltd,** Imperial House, 15/19, Kingsway, London WC2B 6UU. 10 UK offices & 8 overseas offices.

THE HEART OF THE MIDLANDS

Nottingham really is in "The heart of the Midlands" and is conveniently situated at the heart of the UK's communication network. 2 miles from the city centre, 5 minutes away from the M1, 20 minutes away from the East Midlands International Airport – the Centre is in the right place and offers the right sort of facilities and service at the right price.

Before you risk making the wrong choice check us out by ringing Edmund Slicer now for more details and a copy of our brochure.

THE EAST MIDLANDS Conference Centre
University Park
Nottingham NG7 2RJ
Telex: 37346

0602 586565

been ruined because of the reluctance of hall owners to draw this short-coming to the attention of their clients. Some even claim that a test of the acoustics has been made – this 'test' has been done by putting two hands together in a clapping motion, or speaking in an ordinary tone to demonstrate how good the sound is! This so-called test is all very well in an empty room, but it is quite different when the same exercise is repeated in a room full of conference delegates. If in doubt, ask for the name of the previous user and get his comments first hand. In any event, it is important for the venue to ensure that a technician is available – not only for the sound system, but also to be prepared to act immediately should there be any lighting failures or problems with the equipment.

Another point to remember is that of liaison. The person responsible for banqueting will inform you precisely what the venue can do and what its limits are. Identify as quickly as possible the individual at the site who has a track record in terms of the number of similar events handled. If you doubt either the management or the venue's capabilities, ask for names of organisations who have previously held events there. Generally speaking, you will find that companies are happy to discuss their opinions and findings.

A few months before the conference date, it is a good idea to meet the senior banqueting personnel, the electrician and any other personnel involved or playing an important role in the running of the event. There are many instances where the conference will be negotiated and planned with one group of people at a venue site and yet on the day that matters, few are present. Although a great deal can be achieved by getting the paperwork handed over efficiently, nothing will ever replace the need for team participation when putting the event into motion. For that to happen, they should all meet each other, at least once, to talk everything through.

It should go without saying that what you need to do before confirming a venue booking is to surround

4 THE IMPORTANCE OF SELECTING A SUITABLE VENUE

yourself with as much available – and needed – expertise in order to convince yourself that the venue is conducive to the particular requirements of your event. It has to be acknowledged, however, that these procedures are not always adhered to. There is a reason why this does not often happen. People who are organising the conference, and who hold the decision-making capacity, feel that it is beneath them to seek advice. It is essential to be realistic, however; you cannot possibly be expected to know all the answers or to anticipate all the problems that can emerge. Therefore, seek as much advice as you need – after all, it is readily available.

A site selection check list is an indispensable sheet of paper to take with you on site inspections or to have as a reference in your conference file. The check list that follows includes all the basic questions to be asked or ascertained – however, you may wish to add your own to it. One final hint, why not use one check list for each possible venue site to help with comparisons before making your final decision.

Few companies around the world employ full time conference executives; as most companies stage only one or two events annually, this is, of course, understandable. The Case Study that follows, shows the benefit of employing a full or part-time organiser should many conferences be planned (or should they be large ones).

Case Study Company A has offices and representatives in 90 countries worldwide. The president decided that there should be an annual conference of 1,500 employees and that the advertising director should assume the responsibility for choosing the venue. He should also plan the programme, and the overall organisation of the conference. Although successfully employed as the advertising director, he was not qualified for this additional responsibility.

It appeared that the organisation of the conference

would be nothing more than a pleasant interlude. With six months to prepare the event, there was no obvious immediate pressure.

Five journeys to the eventually selected venue meant the advertising director was absent for long periods. As the event grew nearer, memoranda to and from attendees, together with accommodation and travel problems, etc. (not to mention the preparation of the business sessions), meant that the executive was not available to exercise the functions of advertising director. Subordinates lost contact, and the president soon discovered that with each day management and the secretarial personnel in the advertising department became increasingly involved in the administration of the conference.

A long and unfortunate chapter of misadventures at the venue resulted in the dismissal of the advertising director, although the blame was really the company president's for he should have had more foresight. Other similar occurrences are reported frequently throughout the world.

**Case Study
Time spent
in recon-
naissance . . .**

The XYZ Association Conference was destined to be a disaster from the outset. First, the organiser requested an adjoining bedroom for his secretary who accompanied him on his preliminary visit of inspection. Then he seemed more interested in the price of duty-free whiskey than the local experts who were lined up to help him. His attitude towards the hotel manager, the conference officer, and to Guernsey was patronising and dismissive. He knew it all.

Some people assume that, being British, the Channel Islands are just an offshore, VAT-free Brighton or Torquay. He was one of those.

But it was only when the hotel received a copy of his conference programme, a matter of weeks before the event, that the scale of his incompetence became apparent. He was planning an itinerary that was based

4 THE IMPORTANCE OF SELECTING A SUITABLE VENUE

more on the Tourist Guide and wishful thinking than local knowledge or common sense. He was offering his delegates a day trip to Sark on the Sunday – the day that the island is closed – and he was planning an evening barbecue on the little island of Herm when a spring tide would make such a pleasant outing impractical. A welcoming Vin d'Honneur was being given by the States of Guernsey at 6.30 pm on the first evening, but this would be missed by all those delegates who, unaware of it, were booked on later flights.

By the time the hotel received his programme, finding a suitable band for the gala dinner was going to be a problem. His keynote speaker was flying in one hour before his address; allowing no possibility for flight delays. And there were other things destined to trip his conference into chaos.

CONFERENCE GUERNSEY

Many of the best known names in Britain – and on the Continent have held meetings in Guernsey.

Top executive meetings; incentive groups; conferences for over 1,000 delegates; Guernsey can provide all the facilities in a unique atmosphere that's British but abroad.

For full information on meetings in Guernsey please contact:
Michael Paul, Conference Officer, Dept DTC, Guernsey Conference Bureau, PO Box 23, Guernsey, CHANNEL ISLANDS Tel: 0481 26611

Luckily, the hotel manager knew from past experience that if the event was a failure, Guernsey and his establishment would be tainted by association. So he discussed it with the conference officer who, in turn, contacted the organiser at XYZ. Or, at least, he tried to.

The organiser, perhaps seeing the writing on the wall, had resigned and departed; taking his secretary with him. The XYZ Association, blissfully unaware that all was not as it should be with their conference, when the news broke, started to panic. At which point the Guernsey conference officer recommended the services of ACE to them. The Association of Conference Executives is the professional body for the meetings industry and its members are bound by a code of conduct.

Tony Carey, MBIM, Chairman of the Guernsey chapter of ACE.

Finally, you may require further assistance when selecting a venue site. A useful contact is the British National Convention Bureau (0892-33442) which links local authorities, Convention Bureaux and Tourist Boards throughout Britain, the service is free and the advice is impartial. This service is operated through the British Association of Conference Towns

4 THE IMPORTANCE OF SELECTING A SUITABLE VENUE

Site selection check list

- Does the town or city actively solicit business meetings?
- What services does the venue site offer?
- Which airlines serve the local airport?
- What rail and motorway links are there?
- What is public transportation like?
- What is the distance between the company HQ and the site?
- Could the distance between the two create a problem, perhaps altering starting and finishing times?
- What accommodation is available?
- What is the standard of accommodation like?
- Are there other sites close by which could be used?
- Does the town or city have a tourist board who would be able to give advice?
- Are any new facilities planned at the venue site?
- Are there any special cars or buses available?
- What are the costs of:
  room for conference?
  accommodation?
  capabilities?
  extras (list)
- Is lighting and ventilation adequate?
- Are any union negotiations likely?
- Will you have to bring your own AV equipment?
- Is rental equipment up to standard requirements?
- What recreation facilities are available?
- Is the venue's general security arrangement good?
- Any specific areas to avoid?
- How do prices compare with last year's site?
- What local attractions are available for the delegates?
- Is the venue catering good?
- Is the price included in the room hire?
- Should outside caterers be used? If so, who?
- What are local restaurants like? Can they be used for dinner?

5 Choosing the right audio visual medium

What is audio visual? The term means exactly what it says: it refers to a wide range of communication aids – from flip chart and chalkboard, through overhead projection to slides with or without sound, on to film and video, and right up to the most complex and sophisticated mixed-media presentation systems. Whatever form of presentation these audio visual units are used for, these media must always be seen as an aid and never as a substitute or stand-in. Their major purpose is an aid to presentation.

Whether your need is best filled by a simple visual aid or by a professionally produced, pre-recorded programme depends on one thing – what that need is. Do not be misled into thinking that what you have seen some other company do is necessarily best for you. So let this chapter help you find your way to match your needs.

For the sake of convenience, it is possible to divide the entire range of visual and audio visual communication aids into two major blocks: those visual aids where the sound or audio component is likely to be provided by a live presenter, and those using pre-recorded sound.

5 CHOOSING THE RIGHT AUDIO VISUAL MEDIUM

Table 6.

Visual aids	Audio visual or 'AV'
Display material (product display)	Still images: filmstrip with sound single slide with sound two – or three – projector 'dissolve' slides with sound multi-stage slides with sound
Magnetic and other display boards	
Write-on aids e.g. flip chart writing board overhead projector	
	Moving images: Super 8mm film 16mm film 35mm film
Projected aids e.g. slides filmstrip	
Video display of single images	Video images: videotape on monitor(s) videotape by projection videodisc
	Sound and light techniques Mixed or 'multi' media (Many of these AV media can be either back- or front-projected on to a variety of special projection screens.)

But how do you choose the equipment you need? First, concentrate on your objectives and your needs. You may have more than one need – and need more than one medium (e.g. a simple visual aid and a more complex AV presentation system). Do not feel you have to be in the vanguard of technological progress. Remember that yours is a specialist need tailored to a specific and limited audience – your audience. The medium is not the message. What matters is the effectiveness of your presentation, not the technique employed, so wherever possible keep the technology simple.

Asking the right questions may not produce an

absolute, clear-cut answer every time, but it will produce a 'favourite' answer. Your objectives will help point to the single best solution. Table 7 lists different types of meetings and useful presentation equipment.

Table 7.

Visual aid systems for group meetings

If you need:	'Favourite'
1. informal 'once-only' material for informal audience	flipchart/ writing board
2. a teaching session	
3. a mixture of frequently used and specially prepared material	flipchart/ overhead projector/ magnetic board
4. to amend visual(s) during display or presentation	
5. visuals to have same impact and quality as pre-recorded AV inserts	slides
6. material that is easy to prepare 'in-house'	flipchart/ overhead projector
7. on-line computer data to be displayed	video or data projector writing board/flipchart
8. to make presentation in daylight conditions	overhead projector

Audio visual media for presentation to individuals

If you need:	'Favourite'
9. a lot of copies	video/filmstrip
10. only a few copies	slides
11. easy programme-making and amending	slides
12. 'real time' movement	Super 8mm/video
13. best image quality	slides
14. portability	filmstrip/Super 8mm/ single slides
15. low production costs	slides/filmstrip
16. interactive programmes	slides/filmstrip/ videotape

5 CHOOSING THE RIGHT AUDIO VISUAL MEDIUM

Audio visual media for presentation to a group

If you need:	'Favourite'
17. wide (e.g. worldwide) distribution of programme	16mm movie
18. best image quality	slides
19. best sound quality	slide-with-sound/video
20. easy programme editing	slides
21. 'real time' movement	Super 8mm/16mm/video
22. to motivate large audience	16mm/multi-image slides
23. a live presenter to take part	slides
24. reasonable production costs	slides

So far we have made little reference to video because most business meetings depend heavily on charts, graphics, product photographs, etc., and a TV monitor can only show a small amount of information. Projected, large screen video is not yet good enough for still images. But you can transfer from one medium to another, and specialist transfer studios provide these services. However, the transfer must be planned from the start (e.g. a TV screen, 16mm movie and slides have different 'aspect ratios; this means that information – especially typographic – which fits one medium may be cropped when transferred.

Table 8. Media transfers

Single slides to filmstrip (and vice versa)	Easy	Inexpensive
Slides to film	Possible	Expensive
Slides to video	Easy	Reasonable (depends on complexity)
Film to video	Easy	Inexpensive
Video to film	Possible	Expensive

How does audio visual help a presentation achieve its objectives? Very few of us can make a successful presentation – whether to an audience of one or ten thousand – without some sort of planning and

HOW TO SET UP AND RUN CONFERENCES AND MEETINGS

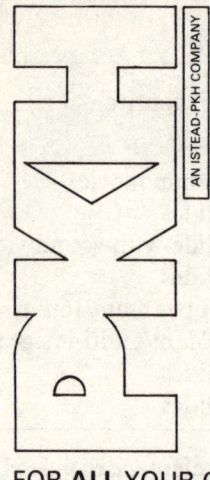

PKH — AN ISTEAD-PKH COMPANY

A NEW CONCEPT FOR BUSY CONFERENCE ORGANISERS.
THE CONFERENCE-INDUSTRIAL THEATRE AND STAGING COMPANY

- Conception
- Planning
- Scripting
- Computer Aided Speaker Support Slides
- Audio Visual Programme Production
- Video Programme Production
- Conference Staging
- Video-Audio Visual-Sound-Lighting Equipment Hire
- Skilled Operators
- Technicians
- Print
- Travel
- Accommodation
- Entertainment
- Rehearsal Facilities

FOR **ALL** YOUR CONFERENCE REQUIREMENTS
Contact: **WENDY TURNER, PKH, SPENCER STREET BIRMINGHAM B18 6DS   021-236 3362**

Westminster AUDIO COMMUNICATIONS LIMITED

- Consultation, supply, installation and operation on a short or long term hire basis of:
- Microphone Management Systems
- Sound Reinforcement
- Simultaneous Interpretation Equipment
- Sound Recording
- Public Address Systems
- Audio Visual Equipment
- Loudhailers
- Mobile P.A.
- HiFi Quality Sound Reproduction Equipment
- Plus a full repair Service for
- Tannoy Loudspeakers
- Amplifiers
- Conference Equipment
- Public Address Systems.

17 Canterbury Grove, West Norwood,
London SE27 0NT, England
Telephone: 01-761 0022/ 01-670 1137
(International) + 44-1761 0022/+ 44-1670 1137

5 CHOOSING THE RIGHT AUDIO VISUAL MEDIUM

preparation. A presentation is almost invariably intended as a formal introduction. It may have any one of a number of possible objectives, but it will usually aim to communicate facts, knowledge and emotion. If presentation demands formality, formality in turn demands discipline. A successful presentation depends, in effect, on a number of 'discipline factors'.

Environment: The right one will help: a poor one will hinder;
Structure: Planning the order in which points are made will ensure that you keep your audience's attention and your audience retains the message;
Content: This must be determined by the agreed objectives;
To-the-Point: 'Going off at a tangent' confuses the audience and devalues your presentation;
Timing: Most of us have only a short attention span; so break the presentation into smaller units (about 15 minutes each);
Pace/pitch: This helps your audience to concentrate by varying the pace and pitch of the presentation;
Rehearsal: All presentations need rehearsal, either in full or – for small in-house events – to check timing and facilities.

The benefits of AV

The idea that using AV or visual aids means less work for the presenter is far from the truth. Initially it will probably mean more work. But, because of the inherent 'discipline factors', AV if used correctly will bring some very important benefits;

— better communication of the basic message;
— greater likelihood that the presentation objectives will be achieved;
— where the presentation has to be repeated several times, AV becomes a time saver and the message is consistent – with no accidental omissions;
— better presentation discipline ensures that your

audience will remember the presentation – and, most of all, its message.

Getting it right

Every good presentation – especially one which involves the use of AV – has a secure starting point when the presenter:

— knows why he is making the presentation;
— knows what he wants to achieve;
— knows his audience and their current level of knowledge on the subject;
— knows what his audience wants from him;
— has selected the right visual and audio visual aids;
— has planned, prepared and rehearsed every part of his presentation.

Objectives

This is where every presentation begins. There must be a clear, coherent and definable objective. Training, selling, motivating, informing – these terms have much in common, but they entail specific objectives. A moody, stylish, up-tempo presentation will probably do wonders for staff motivation: but it is not the best way to provide specific training. Facts and figures will inform, but they are unlikely to inspire.

If visual aids and AV programmes are going to hit their target, you must know where that target is, and why you are trying to hit it. And what you expect your target audience to do once you have 'hit' them. Are you trying to inform or to persuade? To change attitudes or behaviour?

Audience

When you plan to use AV as an aid to communication, it is vital to know your audience. Not just how many will be present, but in particular, what sort of people are they? How much do they already know about the topic/product? How much do they care about it? Will they be able to take any action in response to the presentation? What sort of follow-up will they need? Are they decision-takers or only decision-influencers?

5 CHOOSING THE RIGHT AUDIO VISUAL MEDIUM

Preparation
It is not just a question of getting the objectives and the audience right. Planning and preparation also means choosing the right aids and making sure the presentation has the right overall structure, including variety, pace, natural breaks, etc. It means preparing a full script and making time to have adequate rehearsals.

Organising a script
Any presentation must have a running order or structure; that requires a script – however minimal. Since most business presentations aim to convey facts and figures, the script usually begins as a collection of words. In some cases (e.g. the presentation of the design of a fashion object) the script will begin as a series of visuals. In every case, you should begin by defining your objective and by developing a theme that will achieve it.

Orenamel
Badgemakers to the Famous.

REED employment
DECCA
SEALINK — John Smith
Advance with Albany — JOHN TROY
CRANE FRUEHAUF — DON BROWN
MARLEY Roof Tiles

Renamel conference and personnel badges are made to any size with company name, logo and personal name screened or engraved in your house colours . . . we also carry a range of stock badges which offer easily replaceable name inserts as well as overprinting; plus a wide choice of transparent holders for printed cards.

Renamel has a sound reputation for high quality and attention to detail.

Let us quote you on all your badge requirements.

Renamel Badges Ltd., Cumberland Road, Stanmore, Middlesex HA7 1QH. England.
Telephone 01-204 9522/4 Telex: 8956552 REN.

Some rules for AV

Where a presentation includes some AV 'inserts' – whether they are two minutes or ten minutes long – they must obey some basic rules:

ONE SHOW, ONE MESSAGE: Do not try to make one show do too much. Make two short shows or inserts rather than one that is too long and complex.

KEEP IT SHORT: Eight to ten minutes is the ideal length for an AV presentation. Fifteen minutes is certainly the maximum. For exhibitions and 'single point' shows, no more than three or four minutes.

KEEP IT VISUAL: Avoid the 'recorded lecture'. Make the visuals work for you.

KEEP IT MOVING: Do not allow single images to remain on screen for more than about six seconds each.

The other important point is presenting yourself, and this is covered in Chapter 6.

How are AV programmes made?

An AV programme may be designed to travel around the world – perhaps as a portable video cassette or filmstrip loop – in the sales director's briefcase. Or it may be a more technologically complex, pre-recorded insert designed to slot into the finance director's annual report to shareholders. The range of applications and the number of possible permutations is almost infinite. But whatever the need which the AV programme or show is designed to fill, the questions you need to ask and the procedures to follow are almost always the same.

A few companies and organisations have the capacity to produce AV material in-house: some are capable of doing part of the job; most are not equipped to do more than very basic product work.

The choice is between:

5 CHOOSING THE RIGHT AUDIO VISUAL MEDIUM

— doing all the work in-house;
— doing some of the work in-house and contracting out the rest;
— contracting out the entire production.

The general rule is that unless your company has its own AV production department, it is very unwise to attempt the whole job in-house. Some companies could manage to produce simple training programmes with very few facilities; most users always employ outside production companies to make motivational, sales or public relations shows – wherever image is of great importance.

One reason sometimes given for making in-house production, despite the lack of adequate facilities, is that the information to be disclosed by the programmes is of a confidential nature. Leaving aside the fact that no professional producer would risk his reputation by disclosing his client's secrets, it is perfectly possible for the most confidential information to be inserted into the production at the very last moment – using, for instance, the new 'instant slide' equipment which produces a transparency in about three minutes.

An AV programme – whether slide, film or video based – is the result of a number of specific creative functions. The question is whether any or some of these functions can be fulfilled in-house rather than by contracting out to production companies or facilities houses.

DIRECTING/PRODUCING: In one sense, you are the producer since you are providing the finance. But you may prefer to hire a specialist to direct the entire production or to direct certain aspects (e.g. photographic sessions or sound recording). Most professional directors have experience as an AV photographer or scriptwriter – experience which you are unlikely to find in-house.

SCRIPT WRITING/VISUALISING: It would be a mistake to assume that anyone can write an AV script.

The job entails more than putting words on to a page. The writer must research and analyse the subject from an objective position, devise an overall programme structure, write a script which will sound right and present a detailed visualisation (i.e. ideas for the director and photographer to develop).

AV PHOTOGRAPHY: There are many facets to this job, and you should not assume that a good photographer of one sort (e.g. studio/advertising) can necessarily cope with AV photography. The essence of AV photography is its sequential nature and there are also crucial differences in technique, format and the number of shots to be produced at each location. AV photography also often involves specialist work such as image sequences (e.g. graphics in register) for which it is essential to use a rostrum camera. It is obviously more sensible to buy time from a facilities house than to purchase the expensive equipment yourself.

NARRATION: It is almost always a false economy to use an amateur to supply the voice-over or narration. A professional voice not only gives your programmes the necessary image and authority, but it will also produce a first-class tape in a fraction of the time taken by an amateur.

SOUND STUDIO: Using a professional recording studio will also produce a finished master sound track far more quickly than using an under-equipped, occasionally-used, in-house facility. You may, however, find it useful to assemble a rough version of your programme in-house before spending money on a professional narrator and sound studio. Whichever AV medium is chosen, the procedure for making a programme or presentation insert is much the same:

1. Define objectives – choose medium – agree budget.
2. Prepare first treatment outline – confirm likely costs
3. Write script – prepare storyboard/visualisation.

WE HAVE WAYS OF MAKING YOU TALK

▶ We at Autocue have ways of making people talk like accomplished public speakers. By taking their cue from us, they have no reason to dry up, fluff words or rattle on.

We pioneered Autocueing devices; and the name of our company is now part of the English language.

We offer the widest range of equipment, including computer and colour prompting systems – and back it up with unrivalled, round-the-clock service support. We even offer private rehearsal facilities.

Cue into Autocue for your next conference and you can take it as read that the speakers will never be lost for words. The number to ring is: 01-870 0104. Ask for Steve Powers. ●

AUTOCUE
our name speaks for itself

AUTOCUE HOUSE · 265 MERTON ROAD · LONDON SW18 5JS

4. Location photography – prepare special artwork.
5. Rostrum photography – check script for recording.
6. Record voice-over – prepare sound track.
7. Edit visuals – match sound and visuals – programme/pulse.
8. Preview including client.
9. Produce and supply show copy.

Should you hire or buy?
Your aim will be to get the best out of your investment, and almost certainly that will lead you to choose a combination of outright purchase, term finance and short-term hire. The crucial distinction is between regular and occasional use, between the basic AV infrastructure (e.g. presentation room and projection facilities) and the occasional event (e.g. trade exhibition, sales conference, product launch). You could buy the 'basics' and consider them as an investment to be written off over a period of time (say, four or five years). Then, unless you plan a standard road show to be used several times a year at exhibitions and conferences, you could hire the appropriate equipment. This is not only for financial reasons, but also because when you rent, you can hire the total service including engineers or technicians. You are unlikely to find the necessary staff within your own company to set up, operate and maintain a complex AV presentation.

If you do plan to have your own road show in regular use – and therefore decide to buy rather than hire the equipment – make sure the presentation system is simple enough to be handled by the staff you have – e.g. use a three-projector slide-based system for both the pre-recorded AV components and the visual aids.

Only if you have both the need and the resources to produce at least one AV presentation each month should you consider buying the facilities to make your own AV programmes. If not then 'buy in' either specific services such as script, photography or sound recording studio or employ a production company to supply the entire service. Some visual aids (e.g. 'OHP' transparencies) are more easily produced, and it may

5 CHOOSING THE RIGHT AUDIO VISUAL MEDIUM

well be desirable to set up a small in-house facility for such simple training material. Remember that all AV systems can be hired.

Though leasing or hire purchase is unlikely to be sensible for individual items of equipment, it most certainly is when a major investment is planned, such as the complete system for a presentation or training room, or a range of equipment for the salesforce. Such finance is not available for programme material (i.e. 'software').

The presentation environment

A good environment in which to present your visual and AV material is essential for you and for your audience. You may need to give an AV-based presentation on your customer's premises. Try to get the use of a meeting room rather than an office – especially for a group presentation – and make sure that:

— someone (your contact) has checked the room for blackout, suitable screen, seating, power points, etc.;
— you arrive early enough to set up in comfort;
— you have time for a technical run-through before your audience arrives.

Those same basic – and crucial – rules apply when you are making a presentation on your own premises. But if you plan to take 'presentation' seriously, you will recognise the need for a presentation room: ideally it should be a room used solely for presentations, though in the smaller company it may need also to serve as a boardroom or general meeting room.

Facilities Rather than acquire items of equipment piecemeal, it is advisable to design the presentation room from the outset to 'engineer' the AV system and, if possible, to make one supplier responsible for its successful operation. You will need good blackout and centralised lighting controls. In order to allow a variety of visual and AV systems to be used, the lighting should be 'multi-scene' – so that, for instance, the low light needed for an audience to take notes does not spill on to the projection screen. Because of the high absorption of sound by people and furnishings, even quite small presentation rooms often need some form of speech reinforcement to reduce listener fatigue. The simplest method is to use a lectern amplifier; this should also incorporate the basic room controls (e.g. for lighting and curtains) and simple remote control facilities for slide projectors, etc. AV equipment usually has its own sound system. But if you have several such sources – or a large room – it is worth installing a central audio 'mixing' system.

The audience must be comfortable – though the style of seating will depend on the function of the room (e.g. for prestige visitors or for staff training). They must also all be able to see the projection screen clearly. The number of seats depends on the maximum anticipated regular audience, but the room should feel neither too full nor too empty. It is sometimes necessary and useful to include a product display in the room. This should be lit separately and should not be allowed to distract an audience during a presentation.

In a well-designed presentation room, the audience is unaware of the presence of any technical equipment. They should be interested in the message, not the means. That demands either a separate projection room or back-projection facilities.

1. Projection room: If particular conditions and circumstances oblige you to use front projection, the following points must be taken into account:

— make sure the projection room has a full-width projection window and not just portholes;
— make sure your designer has anticipated the height of the seated audience, as well as any ceiling protrusions or other obstructions.

2. Back projection: This method offers many advantages:

Now, between England and Holland you can stay in a 5 million star hotel.

On Sealink's Harwich-Hook of Holland route, we believe an executive shouldn't be subjected to second class travel just because he's going by sea. Hence our luxury floating hotels: St. Nicholas and Koningin Beatrix.

Check into one of them at Harwich or the Hook of Holland (two ports which are extremely convenient for access within the UK and for travelling to the rest of Europe) and you'll find there's no end to the ways you can enjoy your stay: relax over a drink in the lounge bar. Maybe over dinner in the hotel's exquisite restaurant.

You can have a flutter in the casino. Perhaps a visit to the duty free supermarket. Or a film in the cinema before going to bed for a well earned rest.

And after a good night's sleep a steward will call you in plenty of time to arrive refreshed for that important 9.30 am meeting.

Interested? Then why not take advantage of Sealink's Executive Double H Club. For details ring Harwich (0255) 507022 or 01 834 8122

SEALINK BRITISH FERRIES
Harwich-Hook FERRY LINE

— projection can be used in fairly high ambient light conditions;
— it is easier to mask the projection screen so that it is the right size and format for each presentation;
— where the ceilings are low, back projection allows you to project larger images;
— the audience cannot see any AV equipment.

There are some other points to remember:

— for back projection, special lenses are used which reduce the amount of space needed and eliminate keystone distortion;
— some form of panels or curtain – preferably motorised – should be used to conceal and protect the projection screen when it is not in use;
— where the room is small, you can reduce the amount of space needed by using a 'projection wall' incorporating built-in back projection devices.

In addition to lighting controls, audio and projection equipment, a presentation room should contain a range of facilities including:

— a simple slide projection system;
— the means to show video programmes.

Below is a list of some of the items of equipment you should consider. But remember that a good presentation room is more than the sum of the parts and ensure that the room is designed as a truly integrated presentation facility.

— a single-screen or multi-image slide projection system for the 'house show';
— a 16mm movie projector;
— a teaching wall for training sessions;
— computer graphics projection;
— random access slide projection;
— infra red or 'wireless' control of the room's facilities.

It is very difficult to sell to a large number of people on one occasion. Where this has been done successfully – especially in the travel industry – there has always been a team of staff on hand to 'process' the audience

5 CHOOSING THE RIGHT AUDIO VISUAL MEDIUM

at the end of the presentation. The best opportunity for AV in sales meetings is when the audience consists of a group from one single customer company or organisation. This type of meeting is becoming increasingly important to those with a sophisticated product or service to offer. Such meetings require considerable preparation and organisation.

The use of AV in conferences

There are two main types of conference:

— the sales conference or product launch attended by a group of employees, sales representatives, dealers or customers – people who share a financial interest in the subject matter;
— the general conference (e.g. of a professional association).

Most of the information that follows applies to the sales conference or product launch.

In theory all AV media could be used but in practice slides are the preferred medium because they are best suited to the particular circumstances of a conference (e.g. often some information is not available until the last moment). The same equipment can be used for AV programmes and for speaker support visual aids; slides are bright, colourful and of high quality, and they can be seen clearly by large audiences; slides are the most flexible – they allow for change, addition or new material at the last moment and their projection format and size can be made to fit almost any environment.

You may be uncertain as to which system to use. For the smaller conference, a one-, two- or three-projector system is usually adequate. The larger conference or product launch may in addition consider multivision, with six, nine, twelve or even more projectors – perhaps with movie inserts. The object is to achieve the greatest impact and to produce a large enough image for the whole audience to see comfortably. Modern computer-controlled multivision systems are very reliable and allow a mixture of live and pre-recorded components. They also allow for the inevitable last-minute changes.

The standard slide projector will project a picture up to 15ft wide. Special Xenon Arc slide projectors produce large single images up to 30ft wide, but these projectors are very heavy and very expensive. They tend to be used for the larger, general conference where individual presenters wish to project a few slides or when a single screen programme intended for a few hundred needs to be shown to a few thousand. Many conferences employ the multivision technique in order to present large images (i.e. by using two or three projectors side-by-side on to a wide screen).

Using a television-style prompter allows the speaker at the lectern to appear to know his scripted speech by heart when in fact he is reading it from the prompt image which he can see but his audience cannot. Some speakers prefer to have their key notes on the prompt rather than a complete script.

But when real time movement must be shown, or when TV commercials are to be previewed, film makes the biggest impact. If you need to show a video programme, find out first whether it was originally made on film or slides, and show the original. If you have to use video, a video projector will produce an image up to 9ft wide. It is possible to get an image up to 30ft wide, but the equipment involved is complex and expensive to hire, so you should consider using a number of conveniently positioned linked monitors around the room.

The modern sales conference – often described as 'industrial theatre' – can be a great occasion, so it is crucial that it is well-planned and executed. The cost of the event can be quite small when related to the cost of getting the audience together, and for this reason it is usually best to call in a professional conference producer. You can choose between the theatre-oriented company with the resources to mount a £1 million spectacular car launch . . . and the small producer who understands the needs of the industrial sales conference and will organise all aspects of staging,

5 CHOOSING THE RIGHT AUDIO VISUAL MEDIUM

preparing visuals, making AV models and so on. The sense of occasion is important, and it is possible to hire a complete conference 'set', including lecterns, projection screen with its curtain or panel surround and all other ancillary equipment.

If you employ a professional conference organiser, you should use the experience at your disposal to help you select a suitable venue. But there is no substitute for visiting the venue yourself to check all the details. If a proposed centre or hotel is unable to supply a detailed drawing showing all power points, obstructions and so on, then you may assume the venue is unlikely to be suitable. The minimum requirements are:

— complete blackout;
— dimmer-controlled lighting;
— easy access;
— sufficient room height to allow the use of large projection screen with no obstructions such as chandeliers;
— a good speech reinforcement or public address system;
— unless you are supplying your own set, a good lectern with separate lighting for the speaker – but not lighting the projection screen.

Facts and figures

How much information can be put on a slide? The rule is: keep it simple. Rather than cramming all the information on to one slide, use several slides in sequence. For a standard 35 mm slide (3.2 format):

— do not exceed 40 characters in a full width line;
— do not exceed 14 horizontal lines of text;
— leave at least one full letter height between lines.

As a general rule use no more than 15 to 20 or 25 to 30 figures on one slide. If you want your audience to read and understand the text, it will need to remain on screen for twice the time it takes to read it once – so keep it short as well as simple. Most slide-based presentations use Kodak 'Carousel' slide trays, which take up to 80 slides. Single projector shows should not exceed 80 slides as tray changes during presentation are not recommended. Shows using two or three projectors on a screen can use 160 or 240 slides. (Again, tray changes are not advisable.) A reasonably-paced AV presentation with a recorded commentary will use about 10 slides per minute on the single screen. A slower rate may be justified on occasions by the subject matter, and for motivational shows you may need more than 20 slides a minute.

How much information should be put on an OHP transparency? The rules are much the same as for slides, but here the originals are made full size. Lettering should be at least 0.25 inch (6mm) high.

Most AV programmes can fit within the recommended range of between 8 and 15 minutes. There are occasions when a presentation should be shorter, but no single AV show should ever be as long as 30 minutes. If that length is needed, the material should be divided into two programmes. If you use an audio cassette to carry your programme, use C60 or C90 but not C120.

How many people in a presentation room?
A room about 25 × 32 ft will accommodate up to 45 people theatre style or 25 people schoolroom style. A room about 20 × 25ft will accommodate up to 30 people theatre style or 15 people schoolroom style. If you must cater for up to 25 people, try to ensure the room is at least 20ft wide.

If your conference is being held in an auditorium, as a guideline for theatre-style seating, calculate as minima:

— 3ft or 90cm between rows;
— 21 inches or 54cm seat width;
— 3ft 6 inches or 106cm minimum aisle width.

It is important to avoid seating any of your audience outside a 60° viewing angle (i.e. 30° either side of the centre line), even if this means shorter rows at the front.

5 CHOOSING THE RIGHT AUDIO VISUAL MEDIUM

Another important point to consider is how big the image will be on the screen. The back row of your audience should not be more than eight times the image height from the screen (e.g. for a 6 × 4 ft picture the maximum viewing distance is 32 ft). No-one should be nearer to the screen than twice the image height. (But further back for multivision or 'widescreen').

What lens to use?
To calculate the focal length of lens needed for a given picture size, the formula is:

$$\frac{\text{Focal length of lens in mm}}{\text{Aperture width in mm}} = \frac{\text{Projection distance}}{\text{Screen width}}$$

When working out this formula, do ensure that both projection distance and screen width are in the same unit – either metres or feet. So as to assist, listed below are the most common apertures.

35mm slide	: 35mm
Superslide	: 38mm
35mm Filmstrip	: 22.5mm
16mm movie	: 9.65mm
35mm movie	: 21mm
Super 8mm movie	: 5.35mm

What is the aspect ratio? This is the ratio of picture width to picture height, and the figures given below will help you in defining the screen visibility, as seen by the audience, when using the different types of aperture.

35mm slide	3:2
Superslide	1:1
Movie (16mm or 35mm)	4:3 ('Academy ratio')
Cinemascope 16mm	2.66:1
Cinemascope 35mm	2.34:1 (vanes)
'Widescreen' movie	1.85:1
Video	4:3

And lastly, it is important to know how many feet of film you will need for the programme? Sound film runs at 24 frames per second (when shown on television – 25 frames per second); Super 8mm has 72 frames per foot – so it uses 20ft per minute; 16mm film has 40 frames per foot – so it uses 36ft per minute; 35mm film has 20 frames per foot – so it uses 72ft per minute.

These last few pages are full of useful facts and figures which are necessary for the successful planning of your AV presentation. The subject of this chapter is diverse and as such can be seen as more complicated than the other chapters. But the importance of selecting the right AV equipment cannot be decided without due consideration and planning. So as to assist the reader, a checklist on presentation equipment can be found below.

At the end of this chapter if you still feel uncertain as to what course of action to take, contact the Audio Visual Presentation Advisory Service (AVPAS) who will be able to advise you. For the address and telephone number, please see Appendix III.

Check list. Back to basics

1. Arrange seats and screen so that everybody can see the whole of the picture.
2. Support the projector on a firm stand or trolley.
3. Tilt the screen until the platen projects a square (or rectangle) without converging sides.
4. Try to set the projector-screen distance so that the projected rectangle just overlaps on the black border of the screen. This will mean a slightly greater distance if all your transparencies are in mounts than if – as, for example, with roll film – you are using the whole platen area.
5. Make all these preparations, including putting the spare lamp, pens and transparencies within easy reach, before the audience arrives.
6. Sit while projecting, unless your presentation compels you to leave the projector frequently to do something else.
7. Look at the audience (or the transparency on the platen, but only when necessary), and never glance

5 CHOOSING THE RIGHT AUDIO VISUAL MEDIUM

behind. Unless you are blocking the beam of light, there will be a picture on the screen.

8. Have the lamp on *only* when you intend the audience to concentrate on the transparency.

9. From time to time follow the advice in the instruction book about cleaning the optical parts. The OHP will not be harmed if this is neglected but the quality of the picture, and therefore of your presentation, will.

10. Lastly, do not use the OHP merely for formal presentations. There are other occasions, such as an ad hoc meeting in an office, when it can be a very useful tool.

TIP – Have a spare projection lamp handy during every presentation, unless the projector has a spare built-in (in which event it is wise to make sure beforehand that it works). And do be sure that you know *how* to change a lamp. The procedure may not

---

Advanced Video Hire Ltd.
51 The Cut, London SE1 8LF.
Telephone 01-928 1963

Video Equipment Hire, Long Term Rental, Sales, Facilities and Production

A comprehensive and professional service to trade, commerce, industry and the arts.

- Large quantities of Monitors & Video Projectors including the latest 3 tube Sony multi standard video/data high-quality projector
- Specialists in Computer-Video display including supply of the AVH developed 'Promic' IBM P.C. to video display interface
- Video tape standards conversion and tape copying service
- Comprehensive price list available

Situated within minutes of the City & West End, we are committed to a policy of providing a fast efficient and courteous service, all covered by our 24-hour emergency back up. All service vehicles are equipped with Cellnet telephones.

seem self-evident if you are flustered because the picture has suddenly disappeared. If the projector has a replaceable fuse, tape a spare near the fuseholder just in case a lamp failure causes the working fuse to blow. And never forget that a lamp that fails will be very hot; include a glove or duster in your emergency kit. Keep the new lamp in its sleeve while installing it. If your fingers touch the bulb accidentally, clean it with spirit before switching on.

6 How to hold an audience's attention

The importance of effectively organising a company conference has many different facets but none more important than public speaking – the art of holding your audience's attention. However, before suitable speakers are found, either from within the company or outside, careful thought must be given to the overall objective of the conference and this must play a part in selecting speakers; continuity must be followed throughout. Is the company's objective to create greater public awareness of its product? Or is it seeking to revitalise a sluggish sales force with renewed determination and drive? And what is the overall achievement hoped for from your company's conference?

Once this has been established, you can go on to consider the programme and its length. No doubt you will have seen a number of different venues, and will know what cash has been allocated and how many delegates are anticipated. But do you know the length of the conference, will it need a programme of three hours, five hours or perhaps two days to put across its objectives? This will all influence the number of speakers you invite and the accommodation you will

81

have booked. How many breaks will be needed in the programme? Do not be tempted to try a five hour long stint without a break because you will certainly lose your audience's attention as well as ruin the end objective.

Subject retention is also crucial. Of the 30 to 45 minutes used by each speaker, on average something like one-third of the information given will be retained.

Planning a programme is discussed in Chapter 3, but for the purpose of this example let us assume you are asked to organise the company's annual sales conference with its overall objective to revitalise the sales force's attitude, and also to present a new product before its launch. Let us assume that out of an overall sales force of 25, you have at least 5 new sales people who have not previously met their colleagues, nor the managing director. In all likelihood, they are not too clear on company imagery, public relations or future planning. The sales force is spread across the country so a central location is important when planning your venue location, and in addition the managing director wishes to minimise expenditure on overnight accommodation.

To add to your problems, a certain amount of rivalry exists between the sales department and the marketing department. Your managing director has decided that all personnel who currently come into contact with the customers should attend the one day conference. The chairman has said that he is unable to give the final address and this task has fallen to you!

Working on these assumptions, let us start our planning as in this instance you are the chairperson *and* the organiser. It is likely that you will be able to find two or three speakers within your company, such as the sales director, marketing director and the company's top sales person. In turn, they may want the company's PR consultants to present the new product. You need to ensure that the person knows the conference objectives, and includes them in his or her speech, how the product is to be handled, what the

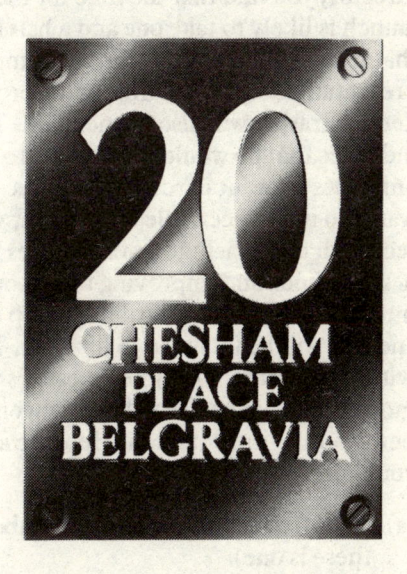

THE SIGN OF A SUCCESSFUL BUSINESS MEETING.

Our beautiful Lyall and Chesham suites provide the ideal venue for you to conduct your business in style. (The Chesham seats 16 for meetings or 50 for cocktails and overlooks a garden square, the Lyall seats 10 or 25 for cocktails.) Both suites are fully air conditioned, with natural daylight. And coupled with delightful food, you could also say it's the perfect setting for any business.

Belgravia-Sheraton

20 CHESHAM PLACE, LONDON SW1X 8HQ. TEL: 01-235 6040
The hospitality people of **ITT**

competition is on the market, any special promotional activities, etc. Having spoken to the marketing director, you find that the time for the new product launch is likely to take one and a half hours; part of that time is to be used by the PR company for their presentation. Question time and a product demonstration will also be included. The sales director indicates that he would like one and a half hours as not only does he want to review the sales situation, but he wants to introduce a sales consultant who, if he is well received, could help to improve sales by introducing new methods and improving on old ones. The sales director will give an award to the top sales person, and this will be included in his time. This leaves you with 20 minutes. The other speakers will cover the motivational drive needed in forthcoming sales and new product introduction. Here are a few ideas for your speech.

(a) To introduce a new senior member of staff (if there is one).
(b) To announce any new plans the company may have, i.e. a new subsidiary.
(c) A brief reference to the history of the firm, recapping on previous speeches and linking through to the new product launch with the success of previous ones.

Remember to keep the speech interesting and lively so that it flows.

Do not forget:

(d) To thank all the guest speakers by name.
(e) To thank the hotel or venue staff and, of course, any company personnel who has helped you.
(f) If the conference is an annual one mention this fact and reiterate how successful they have always been. Always invite delegates to let you know of any particular likes they may have – delegates will always let you know of the problems. Relate an amusing event that happened at the last conference – this usually goes down well.

6 HOW TO HOLD AN AUDIENCE'S ATTENTION

Throughout your speech try to keep control of your physical movements. We all have one common failing. When talking, we demonstrate our words with our hands – sometimes to excess. Movement during presentation is not altogether bad – just be aware of the form it takes. It can be most effective but if used over-much then its whole purpose is lost. The use of facial expression is lost on a conference in a large auditorium, but in a small to medium-sized room, again with limited use, it can be effective. Make a note of your most common actions and see which one has the greatest effect when used for emphasis. If you are able to video yourself making your speech (which is a good idea anyway for the dress rehearsal!) then watch out for your movements, cutting out stilted actions. Lastly, do be conscious of striding up and down the stage. It is most disconcerting for the audience.

Planning your speech

As one of the speakers, you will be anxious to present your speech to the best of your ability. Most people are not used to standing up in front of an audience and so, understandably, their nerves play up. Careful preparation plays an important role in building up confidence, which reduces nerves ensuring that the speech is well presented and received. Your delivery of the speech needs to reflect the subject knowledge you have and the self-esteem necessary to project a positive image.

Everyone has their own style of writing and presenting. This section is not about altering style because that would spell disaster – unfamiliarity can cause confusion. The aim is to put down basic guidelines to follow which can be adapted to fit your general style of speech and presentation. But above all, you must be confident about the subject.

The first important assessment is deciding on what subject area your speech will cover. What are the prime points and what are the auxiliary ones? Commit them to paper for reference. Then start to write your speech.

The basic pattern of speeches consists of:

(a) the introduction;
(b) main body, objectives, etc.;
(c) supporting body; facts, relating other talks or incidences, etc.;
(d) conclusion of speech.
(Both (b) and (c) are interchangeable.)

Draft your speech out first, and read it through several times aloud, noting the length of time it takes and any areas which can be developed. You may find it useful to ask someone to listen or to read through your speech – this is not a bad thing as opinions can be useful assessments. If the speech is running close to its time allocation, do not be tempted to speed up your delivery, instead look at your speech to see what text can be edited out. The speech must be presented in a clear and concise manner so that all can understand the topic or theme.

It is not necessary to open every speech with 'Ladies and Gentlemen, fellow speakers . . .' You could start by saying, 'It is a pleasure to be here today, and to share a platform with such distinguished speakers. Seeing a few of my former colleagues and friends in the audience brings back . . .' You can then do the reverse ending, 'Ladies and Gentlemen, it has been a great honour to be here and . . .' Adapt your speech so that it is punchy and interesting.

Reiteration of an emphatic phrase can add potency and weight to a fact or objective which you are seeking to put across. Placing deliberate pauses of five or so seconds will give your speech added importance. Carefully select a phrase or short sentence that 'trips' nicely off the tongue. A recent speech asking for aid is a clear example: '. . . many millions are starving when they need not. Many millions . . .'

The emphasis was placed on 'many millions', to show the scale of the issue, and each time it was said, the voice level was lifted. The speaker paused between each sentence, hands placed at either side of the podium looking straight at the audience. This

6 HOW TO HOLD AN AUDIENCE'S ATTENTION

combination produced a powerful and well received delivery. But there are other combinations that can be used: voice emphasis can be coupled with physical action too, but be careful about overdoing the latter.

After you have read through your speech a few times and honed it into shaped, go through and underline each key phrase or word which explains the meaning of that particular sentence – a word which you feel would be useful to stress.

It is cumbersome to stand on a podium with sheafs of papers, so if you feel you need some form of *aide memoire* then transfer your important notes on to small cards (4.4 × 6.4in). Clearly write or type your opening remarks and whatever other sentences or notes which you will be using during your speech. Note on the cards at precisely the spot where you wish to refer to slides or films or go to the board to write down key words. Autocues or teleprompters can be used instead of cards.

Whatever remarks are going to accompany pictorial information, keep the copy descriptive, simple and to the point. If you are using slides, as soon as their use is through then take them off the screen – leaving them on view only distracts attention. If you have to refer to the slide further on in the talk then have a duplicate prepared rather than hunting for the precise one later on. Ask for a projector with a remote control so that you are in full control. If this is not possible speak to the projectionist and arrange a signal for a slide change. Try not to look at the slides as this may make you lose your place.

If you are using special drawings make sure that they are suitable for use on a screen. They may need to be redrawn. Keep your version simple, using diagrammatic blocks, lines, etc.: colour also plays an important role as it defines the different areas referred to. Try to translate any tabular information into preferably graphs or diagrams. Draw the graph's flow line(s) clearly or if using more than one line place the rest in different colours. If making up your own slides then make sure you use Letraset or one of the letter prints, do not rely on your handwriting, however neat.

Arrange your audio/visual presentation in its exact sequence and present it as such during the dress rehearsal. Slides should be clean with no dust specks or finger prints showing. On the actual day of the conference, check the film, slide trays and any other visual presentation items you are using. If a projectionist is being used, arrange to go through your requirements at the dress rehearsal (and timing), organising any cues which are necessary.

For the purpose of this next example, we again assume that you are both organiser and chairperson – all things possible rolled into one. Needless to say, you will be a very busy person indeed. Despite this, always discuss thoroughly, with each speaker, the overall theme and objectives of their speeches. In your capacity of conference organiser you should ask what audio/visual equipment they need for their presentation and whether they have used any of it before. All equipment hired or purchased will need to be arranged many weeks beforehand. One week before the conference starts, you will need to have at least one full dress rehearsal with all the speakers and with the equipment in place and working.

Content and participation

The aim of the programme and the speeches is to capture the audience's attention and keep it: to this end, the presentation of material is crucial. The programme should be thought of as a stage performance with the style and pace changing as often as necessary to entertain, intrigue, amuse, surprise and generally capture the audience's attention. Whilst some professional presenters use lasers and smoke screens (even costumes), it is advised to stay away from this pseudo-presentation. Try and strike a happy medium – it can be done. Whilst presentations of extremes are remembered long after the conference, just how they are remembered also needs to be considered as these special effects can also go wrong. I is simply not just a question of pleasing your managing

6 HOW TO HOLD AN AUDIENCE'S ATTENTION

director or 'grabbing' your attendees' attention, but rather of keeping the importance and tone of the conference in mind.

As a conference organiser the need to communicate with all speakers is of prime importance. What are they going to say and do? Talk to each individually (including outside consultants) listening to their ideas, and giving some thoughts of your own (mentally noting possible areas for your own speech). Many a conference has gone wrong when one of the speakers has taken up a pet theme.

Do not forget the benefit of using slides, films, nor the more traditional form of display boards. No matter how intelligent your audience is seen to be, remember the retention and response levels. Make sure that all speakers are aware of it too. Remind them of:

(a) The type of equipment available at the conference;
(b) The different types of presentation.

Different methods of presentation

In noting the different methods of presentation, I will exclude the basic, straightforward speech which is often given unaided. The success or otherwise of this method depends on the speaker and the subject – although response levels do differ with each audience. A good speaker can capture his audience and hold them spellbound by a fascinating subject and an inspirational speech. However, not many of us can be said to be inspirational speakers and if unaided, our speeches can plummet new depths.

1. Type of platform: This influences the way in which the speakers present their material. Should the conference take the form of a symposium or forum then adequate time is needed for the speakers to put forward their different cases and allow the audience to participate actively during question time. Detailed and collective planning is needed should this method be undertaken and it is not recommended for the inexperienced. If a stage is set, the speakers can decide whether to have the floor open for discussion at the end.

2. Visual aids: These include slides, films using overhead projectors, video tapes, flip charts and even boards. If the speaker needs a simple method in order to explain a particular function, then the flip charts and slides would be the most useful. When we move on to videos and films then generally speaking these have to be hired or bought. Visual aids can add clarity to a complicated subject and be an enormous help in keeping the audiences' attention. Chapter 5 gives details on different types of presentation equipment. Depending on the size of the room, back projection is preferable.
3. Physical movement: All of us express ourselves by using different actions, such as hand action, facial expression, etc. During speeches this can become more pronounced. We have mentioned this in previous pages but it is worthwhile reiterating that movement can effectively put across a point while an over-abundance of movement can negate all previous physical emphasis. Watch out for dramatic hand movements as these can easily lead to equipment being knocked over and instead of visual impact can create chaos.
4. Voice: Nerves can play havoc with the vocal chords, paralysing the speaker, or creating a high pitched squeak as he or she utters their first words. There are a few tips which can be given at this stage either for yourself as a speaker or as the conference organiser having to cope with a highly nervous speaker.

If you have a nervous speaker, let them write their speech and then offer to edit it for them. (If nervous yourself, ask someone else to listen to you and edit your speech.) If the speaker is so nervous that he or she cannot remember the theme much less the words, hire a piece of equipment called 'teleprompter': reassure them that there is nothing unusual in using this piece of equipment. Practice makes perfect so let the speaker read his speech a number of times. If possible during the 'dress rehearsal', ask along a few members of staff so that you create an audience. Try and avoid

6 HOW TO HOLD AN AUDIENCE'S ATTENTION

using unfamiliar equipment. Public speaking does dry the throat, so remember to place a jug of water and a glass before each speaker.

5. Demonstration equipment: All platforms will have some form of 'window dressing' from banners and floral decorations to enlarged photographs and products. But some speakers might feel that displays are necessary to demonstrate different processes or new products. In most cases this will mean that a table or stand will have to be placed on the platform with the equipment on it. If all the speakers are on the platform together then ensure that the table is placed nearest the speaker who will be using it, and in such a position that the audience can clearly see the demonstration. All this needs to be prepared for use at the dress rehearsal so that the speakers can rehearse as close to the real occasion as possible.

When briefing the speakers, do make them aware of the details in the programme, and in particular their own start and end times. It is never possible to end a conference right on time but do try to close the conference as near to the proposed time as possible, people may have made appointments or for other reasons may need to get away on time. If you feel that one speaker is going to take longer than others, time the speech at the dress rehearsal and either ask the speaker to reduce the length or allow in your programme an extra 5 or 10 minutes.

Every conference has one speaker who never finishes on time. If you are aware of this before the start then an additional allocation of time is perhaps the most tactful method to use. Arrange a signal to catch the eye of the speaker to tell him when the period is coming to a close – but do not interrupt during the speech. On the other hand, you will have speakers who finish early. If you have run over the time, then this will be thankfully received especially if you are running towards a short break. Many a good chairperson prepares an amusing extra anecdote which can be used, if necessary, at such moments to fill the time gap. A question or two illicited from the delegates is another method. (You may wish to have these in reserve.)

Guest speakers

Public speaking holds a certain fear for us lesser mortals and if we can pass the task on to someone else then we will do so – sometimes this delegation is made easy. However, if you have to choose, then draw up a short list of suitable people. Naturally, there are certain criteria to follow when doing this. Firstly, they must be good speakers and secondly, they must have a knowledge of the subject or be a recognised person in their own field. A well-known personality is often a great bonus at a product launch – someone who the audience feels they can associate with.

Before you approach these potential speakers, be aware of what they charge for public appearances, this can be anything between £150 and £1,000 and in some cases much more. You should have an idea of how much you are willing to pay for an appearance. Your PR or marketing department may be able to advise you or to check out beforehand who charges what. You will have to pay all the guest speaker's expenses which may include accommodation and most certainly transport.

It is best if the proposed guest speaker is first approached on the telephone, given as much information as possible and answering any queries he or she may have. Once an agreement has been reached, confirm it in writing, noting all arrangements, fees, expenses, objectives (and theme, if any) of the conference. Organise a meeting and thoroughly brief the guest speaker making sure he knows who he will be sharing the platform with, the topics of other speeches, etc. Detailed arrangements such as location, time, programme, etc., should also be committed in writing, followed by a telephone call nearer the time.

Ask the guest speaker to come along to the dress rehearsal 'to meet the other speakers and familiarise himself with the theme and surroundings'. If he is able

6 HOW TO HOLD AN AUDIENCE'S ATTENTION

to do this, then you will have to pay him for time and expenses too. On the day of the conference, meet all the speakers and introduce them to each other and to any company dignitaries who are present.

Rehearsals At least one dress rehearsal should be organised, usually one week before the conference and at the venue site. Any presentation equipment which is needed should be there and in working order. This allows time for any script changes; some slides may need re-doing, and even the set may need alteration. So allow yourself plenty of time.

In ideal circumstances, the conference organiser will not be the conference chairperson. If this is the case then a full briefing needs to be given at each stage to the chairperson. Indeed, he or she can be an immense help maybe even suggesting a suitable guest speaker, or even organising that part of it for you.

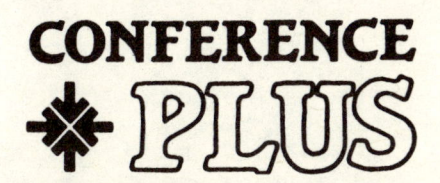

CONFERENCE ✦ PLUS

An organisation of particularly skilled people with a wide experience of the hotel and meetings business.
We provide a personal, friendly and efficient service to the Conference Organiser including:–
★ Free venue finding service
★ All aspects of conference planning
★ Organisation and management of meetings
★ Motivation travel schemes in this country and abroad
We tailor our services to your requirements.
Telephone: David Selby on (0926) 833388 – Midlands London South
or   Jill Denardo (0298) 79355 – Northern England and Scotland
Conference Plus Ltd. 8 Portland Street, Leamington Spa CV32 5HE

The chairperson needs to be familiar with all company related aspects. The role he or she plays could be described as the 'guiding hand', introducing speakers and signalling for any breaks. There are two key platform roles at any conference, one is the chairperson and the other is the guest speaker. As organiser you have a choice of both. The guest speaker needs to be interesting and enthusiastic and the chairperson needs to be diplomatic.

7 Further planning considerations

It cannot be over-stressed, the way to achieve a successful conference is organisation – and organisation takes time. Weeks ahead or even a couple of months ahead is not sufficient time to make arrangements and complete the organisation of all the necessary conference ingredients. Afterall, you are not a professional conference organiser and have other work to do in addition to your company's conference planning (see the graphic example in Chapter 4). So what, you may ask, are all the necessary arrangements? Well it means the obvious, ensuring that the delegates know where they are going and on the right day. The main planning items, such as venue booking, accommodation, catering, inviting delegates, tend to overshadow other smaller administrative duties because technically, they can be seen as the mechanical element of conference planning. Therefore this chapter looks at all the smaller items, the incidentals, which can play a crucial role in the successful organising of a conference.

In an ideal situation there will be the conference organiser who handles all the administration, together with the conference back-up team, and the conference chairperson. But often, because of time and other commercial constraints, one person is appointed with perhaps an assistant to help. Small meetings can get away with one person organising everything but large events do need extra hands, especially if your time is not solely dedicated to this task.

Meetings take a great deal of time, care and patience to organise and the event cannot be conjured up overnight. If you have been left with an unreasonably short period of time, then do make it known and ask for assistance or a postponement – it may be a noble act to battle on, but when the event turns sour, you will be blamed. As a rough rule of thumb, allow yourself at least four months to organise a small event (30 or so delegates), but more time will be needed for larger events or if the content of the conference is detailed. When next you receive a leaflet telling of a specialist conference being held, stop and look at the date, then add on some four to six months prior to the mailing of that leaflet – just to give you a rough idea of the time needed to plan and organise. It does make your own timescale pale into insignificance!

Successful conference administration in the first instance means a mound of paperwork, sending and receiving letters, file notes, discussion documents and the like. All should be *typed* – please do not rely on hand-written notes!

Your first organiser's meeting should be minuted and copies circulated to all present and to those directly involved but who were not present. It goes without saying that the task will be that much easier if your company possesses a wordprocessor, and you have use of it. If you are still a non-believer, let us add a few more instances to our list. Other than minutes of meetings, letters to speakers, letters to all delegates, lists of attendants of both speakers and delegates, confirmation letters to venues, letters to hire companies, caterers, translators or interpreters (depending on your needs), all have to be produced, signed and mailed out.

Conference organising is the meshing together of

7 FURTHER PLANNING CONSIDERATIONS

many elements. And each has to be organised in the right sequence. A calendar has been prepared giving a lead time of 12 months for a one day conference. You may even add a few extras to this list.

So much can depend on how much notice you have been given to organise the event. Far too frequently companies proceed with their meeting having only given six to eight weeks notice. Longer periods of time would be appreciated by the organiser and should be asked for.

Conference timetable

This list covers a twelve month period. If your time allocation is shorter, or longer, then the time sequence will need adjustment. Try to work back from the date of the proposed meeting as you will have a better idea of any existing time constraints.

Month 1
— Policy decision;
— Appointing conference organiser and/or committee;
— Agree a theme for the conference/exhibition;
— Plan promotional policy.

Month 2
— Visit suitable conference locations and accommodation;
— Discuss with them any added extras which may be needed and which they supply;
— Agree with directors the number of attendees;
— Organise any advertisement or PR implications;
— Prepare with directors and managers a guest list;
— Prepare staff list;
— Agree both the guest list and staff list;
— Check estimates off against your budget.

Month 3
— Select the right location;
— Plan conference literature;
— Discuss any display material needed;

— Organise insurance cover;
— Discuss any video presentation equipment needed.

Month 4
— Double check the room size and number of attendees;
— Test video equipment and then book it;
— Organise any secretarial or stand assistance;
— Contact guest speaker(s).

Month 5
— Prepare any pre-conference/exhibition literature (including map of location);
— Order tickets and badges;
— Plan any presentation, i.e. gifts, etc.;
— Order gifts;
— Book hotel accommodation.

Month 6
— Mail out conference/exhibition details to all staff attending and guest speakers letting them know that further information will be coming in due course;
— Organise any transportation necessary;
— Plan catering and entertainment;
— Ensure that hotel and delegates know who pays for what.

Month 7
— Organise pre or post conference catering;
— Draw up a seating plan for both the conference and pre or post entertainment;
— Check any advertisement copy and PR copy needed;
— Discuss and organise display stands;
— Book any transportation needed.

Month 8
— Visit location again to re-check facilities;
— Send advertisement copy out;

7 FURTHER PLANNING CONSIDERATIONS

- Send out transportation tickets along with any necessary details;
- Print conference/exhibition literature.

Month 9
- Mail further information to guests and delegates including map of location, request an RSVP;
- Double-check conference room for revised seating as well as for presentation equipment;
- Arrange any extras such as flowers for guests;
- Send a final list of attendants to conference centre and/or hotel.

Month 10
- Collect printed literature;
- Go through final plan with the conference committee and/or your assistant;
- Final confirmation with guest speaker(s);
- Brief conference chairman.

Month 11
- Final confirmation of seating plans for conference/hotel;
- Catering – send details to site and also accommodation point: also to chairman, committee and assistant;
- Collect gift or presentation;
- Send out any final details or instructions.

Month 12
One week before – Dress rehearsal
- Stay at the hotel and visit the conference centre re-checking all arrangements;
- Arrange display material;
- Set up video equipment;
- Check seating and catering arrangements;
- Familiarise the projectionist with the equipment and the materials.

D-Day
- Lay out badges and any table arrangements needed, also put up any banners and displays;

— Meet guests and delegates;
— Introduce conference chairman;
— Explain any last minute alterations to conference or entertainment;
— Reception – seating: presentation.

D-Day plus
— Dismantle display;*
— Take down equipment, check it against your list and return to supplier(s);*
— Pack surplus literature;*
— Final check with hotel and conference centre;
— Check invoices;
— Compile a report on the success of the conference;
— Discuss future conferences.

*The first three items may need attention immediately after the conference.

Pre-conference literature

The aim of any printed matter sent out prior to a conference, is to advise and inform. Speakers and delegates should know at least three to four months before the conference, where it will be held and the date. There have been cases where delegates arrived for a conference a week before it actually took place, incurring additional expense.

What should the pre-conference literature contain? The venue site will, in all likelihood, have a map printed showing its exact location. Ask if this can be used, if not make up your own. A friendly, informative letter should be sent out to all attendants telling them as much information as is currently available (speakers, venue, objectives, how to get there, accommodation, length of conference, etc.), and in an easily digestible form. The sales director (or marketing director) may want a new company brochure sent out with this information pack, or if a new product is to be launched shortly, the marketing director may wish to advise the 'front-line' sales team. Badges can also be sent out early. Pull together an attractive package to initiate interest and response.

TIP – If maps have to be printed, always print more

7 FURTHER PLANNING CONSIDERATIONS

than are needed as they, as well as badges, have a tendency to get misplaced.

Conference packs
Handouts at a conference are usual but it depends on the conference format and the programme as to whether these are handed out in presentation packs (as delegates enter the conference) or in the form of individual papers handed out during the conference. This latter method may seem clumsy, but if you are launching a new product under strict security, with an embargo in force, then it can be useful. Whatever printed material is required, arrangements have to be made allowing adequate time for printing and delivery.

TIP – Always double-check any artwork for accuracy before sending it to the printers. And check that conference packs are taken to the event. Many is the time that these have been left back at the office.

Conferences & Exhibitions International Diary 1987

This magnificent diary is a must for the Meetings and Incentive Travel executive. The new CEI 1987 Desk Diary combines prestigious looks with an easy to read layout. It gives a week-at-a-glance format and provides essential reference information for the professional meetings organiser.

Among the vital information in the diary, you'll find a colour world atlas, street maps of many major cities throughout the world, contacts lists of meetings organisations worldwide plus contributions from leading experts on the latest trends and developments within the industry.

The diary can be embossed to your order with initials, a complete name or even a company logo. The 1987 CEI Diary is not only an invaluable business aid but an ideal gift.

For full details write to:
Gill Jones
International Trade Publications Ltd.
FREEPOST
2 Queensway
REDHILL
Surrey
RH1 1ZA
Or telephone Redhill (0737) 68611

CEI
CONFERENCES & EXHIBITIONS INTERNATIONAL

Diary 1987

Badges

Along with conference packs, badges can be given out as delegates enter the room.

Ask your supplier to provide you with different samples; get opinions from colleagues as to which they prefer. Try to avoid badges with safety pins as they can damage clothes. Badges which have a stick-on backing are fine for one-day conferences but are not suitable for longer events. Badges with clips and pins are available. Badges should be durable enough to last the event and those with plastic covers tend to wear well.

Have delegates' names printed on the badges; if you leave them blank then delegates will have to print their names on – and not everyone's writing is legible. If you are going to print names on the badges, then make sure that individuals and company names are spelt correctly.

TIP – Badges can show their own brand of individuality and be reasonably priced too. Why not have your company's logo or name printed across the top. Also remember to order spare badges to hand out at the meeting.

Banners and other promotional display material

Display material such as banners and sashes do look attractive. But before you rush off to have a banner printed 'THE WIDGET GIDGET CONFERENCE' check with the hotel to see if it is all right to have them displayed. Having said that, most hotels and conference centres will give you the go-ahead to display company brochures, banners, and even small pieces of equipment. The latter does add a nice touch to any conference display but check that this is possible and that the equipment can fit into the display with easy access to and from the display. Before going ahead and committing your firm to extra expense, take the advice of your marketing or advertising department as they may have most, if not all, of your display presentation material.

TIP – If acceptable to the location, try and prepare a

7 FURTHER PLANNING CONSIDERATIONS

display presentation area just before or surrounding the entrance to the conference room. A nice touch can be added, if the venue site is able to fly the company's flag.

Sign posts

If you are organising an event in a large and unfamiliar venue, neatly print little cards saying 'WIDGET GIDGET CONFERENCE' with an arrow pointing towards the location. If private parking has been agreed, it is useful to place a sign stating that these spaces are reserved for conference attendees.

Travel and accommodation

There are very few conferences which do not require the organising of travel and accommodation. Guest speakers will need both travel and accommodation arrangements made (and paid for by the firm) on their behalf. If your conference is an inter-company PR exercise spread over a couple of days, then attendees may be invited to bring along their spouses. Ask all attendants to let you know beforehand what accommodation requirements will be needed. Overseas arrangements are discussed in Chapter 9.

If the company is not prepared to pay for drinks, telephone calls, etc., then make sure that the hotel knows what to charge the company for, and that the delegates know what is included and what they will have to pay for. This information should be noted in the pre-conference letter. You may find that the venue site will run two accounts.

Insurance cover

Venue sites usually have a basic insurance cover, say, if a delegate trips up over a loose bit of carpet and ends up breaking an arm. But you should insure for loss of equipment through theft or fire, and most certainly include for the possible cancellation of the event itself.

Insuring for loss is an essential part of any conference organiser's duties and the sooner the arrangements are made (in writing), the easier your mind will be. And in case of cancellation or abandonment, the company will not lose out on expenses incurred.

The company may have an insurance broker who they deal with, tell him what cover is needed and ask him to supply quotations. The insurance cost will depend on the number of delegates, the venue, and what cover you require, 'All risks' or 'standard'. A conference insurance specialist in this field is Robertson Taylor Insurance Brokers Ltd, Millard House, Cutler Street, London E1 7DJ (01-283 3956). Another insurance plan is ACEPLAN (recommended by ACE International) and details can be obtained from Expo-Sure Ltd, The Pan Files, Tunbridge Wells TW2 5TH (0892-39506).

Secretarial and administrative assistance

Whatever happens, you will need secretarial and administrative assistance at the very start of the conference, most certainly towards the end, and on the day of the conference.

Before the start of the conference, delegates will be telephoning to request another copy of the map or to ask again about travel and accommodation arrangements (although a letter should have been sent out confirming arrangements). You may be out of the office double-checking equipment, meeting speakers, or on other company business. So you will want a reliable person to process any such queries that come in.

On the day of the conference, no matter how professional you are, problems will occur. You will be pulled in all directions but the fundamental duties will still need to be carried out. These duties include welcoming the delegates at the door of the conference room, checking their names off the delegates list and sorting out any queries they may have. Meanwhile, refreshment arrangements will need to be checked, a double-check will need to be done on the microphones, a check made to ensure that the electric plug is switched on for any visual presentations. And

7 FURTHER PLANNING CONSIDERATIONS

so the list goes on! You cannot be in all places at the same time – so do get some assistance.

TIP – Having an assistant will give you more time to mix with the delegates and to get a first-hand reaction as to how they feel the conference is going.

Translation and interpretation	In the event that overseas delegates will be attending, and assuming that their command of the English language is not sufficient to sit through and understand every word of a new product launch, then it is important to hire (at least three months beforehand) an interpreter, preferably whose mother-tongue is the foreign language. You will also need to ask speakers to send in typed copies of their speeches beforehand. These will need to be copied and given to the translator and the interpreter, if one is working at the conference; brief both as to the overall theme of the conference, what it hopes to achieve, and go through each speech with the interpreter.

If you are holding an informal small meeting then it is not necessary to organise a separate room with communication equipment. However, if you are organising a large conference, then it becomes necessary to use a separate room and install the necessary equipment. Checks need to be made that the earphones are working; explain to the guest speaker or delegates how to use the communication system. If overseas government delegates are attending they often bring their own interpreter with them.

Check with your local yellow pages for a translation or interpretation service or contact your local chamber of commerce. Advice and information can also be obtained from the Simultaneous Interpretation Equipment Suppliers Association (9 Hesper Mews, London SW5 0HH) on 01-373 9474.

Equipment hire

Presentation equipment
This is covered in detail in Chapter 5, but you will need to know a few months in advance what

presentation equipment is required by guest speakers, and what is part of the package offered by the venue location.

Confirm your booking of any equipment in writing, specifying the date you wish to collect, the day it will be returned, and the charge. The hire company will probably insure their own equipment but it would be a wise precaution to check this and if in doubt, include it on your company's conference insurance plan.

TIP – Collect the equipment the day before the dress rehearsal so that it can be used the following day. Should there be a malfunction then this is found out at an early stage and can be corrected. Make a check list of all equipment hired or bought.

Films/videos/slides, etc.
Films and videos are a useful addition to a conference and can be hired at a reasonable price. But again, prior notice of booking has to be given and a check made with the lessor as to what type of equipment is needed.

Again, have the films or videos sent leaving enough time so that checks can be made during the dress rehearsal. Speakers may supply their own slides or they may ask you to obtain them. Make sure that the speaker has checked that the slides are in the correct order before being used. This is a common mishap and one which can so easily be averted.

Lighting
Should you wish special lighting or special effects then it is unlikely that the venue location will be able to help. Specialists firms will need to be contacted. But do obtain references and check them out first.

Venue point

Different arrangements will need to be made at the venue point; listed below are the less obvious ones.

Conference registration point
Ask the venue location to supply a table, suitably covered, and two chairs: place these furnishings at the

7 FURTHER PLANNING CONSIDERATIONS

door to the conference room. On the day of the meeting, station your assistant there and request that all delegates' names be ticked off from the list as they arrive. Badges and conference packs can also be handed out.

Layout of room

This is very important and should have been organised well in advance. Delegates must have a clear and unhindered view of the podium and not have to dodge floral arrangements or columns in order to see the stage. If an overhead projector is being used at the back of the room, ensure that its placement is such that heads do not get in the way. The image being projected should fit exactly on the screen. When hiring the equipment, tell the supplier the dimensions of the room, the screen and its placement (see Chapter 5). Easy aisle access is also important as much for safety as for comfort. Seating should not be cramped and there should be reasonable leg-room.

Heating and air conditioning

When 20 to 30 people are together in a room, after two hours the air may get musty and stale. If the meeting is being held during the winter months, see whether adequate provision has been made for ventilation and heating and in the summer, air conditioning.

TIP – Either segregate the smokers to the back of the room or near to the ventilation point. Alternatively, request that no one smokes in the conference room.

Message points

Again use your registration point to collect and disburse messages. Instruct the venue location to pass all messages on to this point.

TIP – Ask the venue location to put an extension on your front desk for easy communications. If a telephone has to be put in the conference room, ask that no calls be put through during the duration of the sessions. Carry out technical as well as catering survey trips – do not rely on the venue's brochures.

Telephones and other communication services

Allowing delegates free use of the telephone can be a costly business and if you do not wish an enormous bill at the end, brief your assistant to advise delegates of the facilities and their location. Telexes may need to be sent (or received) and arrangements need to be made.

For conferences that last over two days, further room may be needed for a mobile administrative office. This will have to be hired.

Lost and found

Instruct the venue to collect and keep all items found at the end of the conference. If large items are found, a charge may be incurred for their return. You can try and recover this from the owner.

Noise levels

High levels of noise can be very disruptive during a meeting. If a new wing is being built at a venue site then do ask the site manager or the venue manager to curtail the noise while the conference is in progress. It is worthwhile checking before you hire the venue to see if any alterations, both internal and external, are likely to be underway during the time the conference is being held.

Security

Sadly in the light of recent occurrences, security arrangements have now to be considered, especially if you are holding an overseas conference in a high risk area or if a prominent person is attending. The venue may have its own search procedure but if they do not, it is worthwhile organising this as a separate item. If you do, please allow adequate time and forewarn delegates.

The venue location will have made provisions for emergencies (including bombs, fire, etc.). Make sure that the conference room has adequate exits and that they are clearly marked. Also inform your assistant and the chairperson of the arrangements.

7 FURTHER PLANNING CONSIDERATIONS

Industrial espionage

Spies are not just found in books and films, industrial espionage is a very real threat. If you are launching a special project, which you feel your competitors will want to know about, then do engage a security consultant. The conference room will have to be swept for bugs and a close watch put on any material that might be sensitive. Strict security, allowing only cleared personnel into the security zone, will also need to be enforced. But before implementing any of these drastic procedures, do check that they are really needed!

Extras

Spare equipment

If your conference is very large or if it is over a few days, then it may be worthwhile to consider hiring spare equipment in case of breakdown. There again it may not be necessary if the hire company has guaranteed (in writing) that the equipment will be replaced within one hour at their own expense.

Photographs to record the event

Your marketing department will be able to help organise official photographs. They may even take the task on themselves so that the photographs or video film can be used in future promotions. Be clear about who is organising what!

Extra conference staff

You may feel that more assistance will be needed on the day, or that products will need to be demonstrated and so on. Organise extra staffing requirements well beforehand, gaining permission from the staff and their supervisors. Transport for these 'extra' hands will need to be planned, and if necessary accommodation; thoroughly brief staff on the venue location, the duties and the overall aim of the conference. They should be suitably dressed and briefed on what to say. Ask staff to note any reaction expressed to them on how the conference is seen by delegates.

Dealing with the press

If launching a new product, then dealing with the press should be handled by the company's public relations manager or marketing manager. The managing director may also wish to get involved.

Pre-plan with the person responsible for the press launch. It might be more convenient to hire an additional room where literature, telephones and the relevant company personnel are available to answer any questions. Invitations should be sent out three to four weeks beforehand, requesting a RSVP. Try to have the event in the middle of the week; both Mondays and Fridays are not very good days. Follow up the invitation a few days before the event to check that delegates will be attending. Do not promise to send off a press release until after the event as this may persuade them that life could be a lot easier not attending.

---

oxford polytechnic
offers you

all the resources of an establishment of Higher Education at reasonable cost. With two teaching sites just 1 mile and 6 miles from Oxford City Centre and good road and rail access from London, Birmingham and the South West, Oxford is the ideal conference location.

If you come to Oxford Polytechnic for your conference or course you will be provided with a range of teaching facilities and aids, good single study-bedroom accommodation and an interesting range of catering options.

Residential courses can be accommodated during December/January, April, July, August and September. Facilities for non-residential courses may be requested at any time of the year.

For further details contact – Peter Ledger,
Conference and Lettings Officer,
Oxford Polytechnic, Gipsy Lane,
Headington, Oxford OX3 0BP
Telephone: Oxford 64777 (Ext. 626)

oxford polytechnic

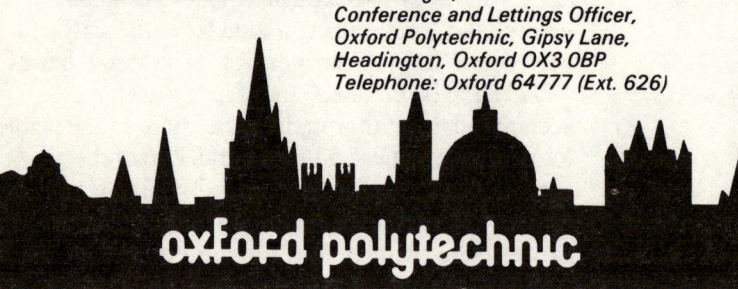

7 FURTHER PLANNING CONSIDERATIONS

Distributing conference papers
It may be useful to hand out conference papers before or at the close of the conference, and if this is the case, speeches will have to be collected well in advance and printed. Make sure that each speaker sends in *typed* copy, which has been checked, and that they all have a house style sheet to follow for conformity of style (the way to present different types of headings, etc.). Permission to print their speeches will need to be sought *before* the work is printed.

8 Conference catering

By now you are probably feeling a bit punch drunk anticipating 'decisions, decisions' facing you at every turn. And you are right. Here is yet another phase to add to your list of decisions – conference catering. Even if you want to keep the conference to the simplest possible level, catering will still have to be planned and agreed – it will all depend on the conference, the programme (and its duration) and the number of people. All refreshments should be planned to fit in with the conference programme, and as we have said before, well organised breaks can form a vital part in the programme to revitalise and refresh delegates. So what should be served? Who does the catering – the hotel or conference centre catering staff, outside catering contractors or, should your company have its own catering facilities, perhaps company catering staff? But whoever does the catering, decisions will have to be made as to suitable menus, programmes will have to be checked for suitable breaks and refreshments periods; most important of all, the final number of delegates will need to be known and the figure given.

The approximate number of delegates will be

8 CONFERENCE CATERING

known beforehand and the catering manager should be advised of this number as soon as it is known: if possible, tell him the final figure one week *before* the conference start date. Should your chairman or managing director be the sort who brings along extra people unannounced, then to save a lot of aggravation add on a few extra 'heads', say two or three, so that you are not caught short-handed. This is all right if you are paying an '8 hour day rate' based on a 'per head' charge (extra cost approximately £65) or where you are paying a menu 'per head' rate (costing between £12 and £15 depending on the choice of menu). However, if closely watching costs, do not even think of adding on the extras if you are paying a '24-hour rate' (which includes overnight accommodation) as a minimum it would cost an extra £195 for an additional three attendees. Careful thought is needed as extra numbers can be very expensive.

Any uncertainty about actual numbers should be treated with caution, and if there are not many delegates attending, give an approximate number and try to put off the final count until the actual day. An added help in the final analysis of numbers can be given by the delegates' registration desk – but do not forget to add on guest speakers and other members of staff!

Where will these refreshment breaks be held – possibly in an adjoining private room or in the hotel's lobby or coffee area? Privacy may be an important factor in which case an adjoining room should be hired. But this is where the inspection trip helps as you are able to see other possible solutions, for example, a corner of the coffee shop reserved for your firm – or your group may be small and the lobby may be extremely large. But agreement to do this has to be reached with the hotel's conference manager. Wherever the location, outside caterers must be told where refreshments will be served so that they can prepare (and all staff helpers, delegates and speakers must be aware of its location on the day). If utilising the catering facilities at a hotel or conference centre, discuss all arrangements with the catering manager who should ensure that things run smoothly.

Different types of catering

Hotels usually have special conference packages. These can be a basic 'day rate' (8 hours) or a 24-hour conference which includes overnight accommodation. Costs are based on a 'per head' rate and any extras are added to the bill. You can, however, hire a conference site and lay on the extras yourself but how these affect costs will depend on many factors. If the conference venue site is different to the accommodation then this will add to your costs. A typical rural four-star hotel charges between £60 to £65 per delegate for a 24-hour conference (plus VAT, any extras or alteration to their stated menu plan). For this the company hires the conference room for the day, morning refreshments, three-course lunch, afternoon tea and evening dinner (table d'hôte). The delegate is offered overnight accommodation and English or Continental breakfast the next morning. By comparison, a day rate, based as above example, would cost approximately £20 per delegate and this price includes a three-course buffet lunch, afternoon tea with biscuits, hire of the conference room (plus VAT, any extras or any alteration to stated menu). Doing it the third route, hiring a separate venue site from the hotel, would mean costing out each item separately, but you would be able to order exactly what you required.

Let us look at the three stages of catering that complement the standard conference. The first one is the refreshment break where tea and coffee is served. These breaks can fill gaps as well as their prerequisite function. These refreshments should ideally be centrally located. Earlier on in the book we cited an example where a refreshment break was used before the start of the conference. It filled two important roles. In the example, delegates were arriving from different parts of the UK, and although a specified start time had been given, delays occurred. The extra time allowed the conference to start on time with all

8 CONFERENCE CATERING

the delegates present and the break saved any interruption of the conference after it had started. Interruptions during the conference must be avoided at all costs. The second benefit gained from this extra time was one of communication – it gave fellow delegates and speakers a brief chance to mingle and to talk with each other before the conference started; a pleasant and friendly atmosphere had built up from the very start.

These refreshment breaks need not be elaborate affairs. Coffee and tea should be provided, perhaps fresh orange juice, biscuits or even pastries can be laid on. They can, however, create one problem for the conference organiser – timing. Try and keep as close as possible to the time specified in the programme. If there are four breaks during the conference and you are late by ten minutes or so each time then this puts pressure on your schedule.

Even if your company's conference is only a short one, with limited expenses, some form of meal should be provided. This may be at midday or later on, perhaps in the early evening. As a simple rule of thumb, should the meal take place before the conference or in the middle of the day, then light meals should be served, meals that are quick and easy to serve with perhaps a glass or two of wine but nothing more. You do not want delegates nodding off during the conference due to rich food and plentiful drink. More sumptuous menus can be planned for pre-conference or after-conference dinners.

Find out beforehand whether any delegates or speakers are vegetarian or belong to a religious sect that lay down special rules; then again, a delegate may be on a special diet for health reasons and this should also be observed. Do not, however, become chained to this cause. As you will be sending a letter to all delegates advising them of the conference venue, location, etc. well beforehand, place a footnote on the letter asking them to reply by 'XX March 19XX' stating whether they are vegetarian or for health reasons need a special menu and to let you know in writing what is required. Remember that you may have to pay extra for these non-standard meals.

When you have got all your facts together go along and talk to the venue's catering manager (or to your own). The standard menus for the day rate (or 24-hour rate) may not suit your requirements, although they are the easiest to organise, if so ask the catering manager to suggest a few menus and to cost them out for you. He may suggest that instead of a served meal, a finger buffet may be more suitable. (See possible menu examples, with costs, later in this chapter, but remember prices do alter from location to location.) These specially selected menus will be costed at a 'per head' price, in other words, what each menu will cost per individual delegate: finger and fork buffets are the cheapest and waiter service is the most expensive. Drinks are added to the bill on a per bottle rate. Try and agree a set amount of bottles of wine before the start of the meal, the catering manager will advise on

NEWCASTLE UPON TYNE
undiscovered pleasure
come and see for yourself!

A MODERN CONFERENCE CITY WITH A RICH CULTURAL HERITAGE

The capital city of North East England, standing on the banks of the Tyne, set against the back-drop of the Northumberland National Park provides an original and ideal venue for your next conference.

Our excellent facilities are epitomised in our modern Civic Centre, and Europe's busiest and most up to date enclosed shopping and recreation centre, Eldon Square.

We reckon the friendly people, the very many comfortable hotels, guesthouses, Polytechnic and University accommodation, and arguably the best entertainment outside London, will make your visit a memorable one.

To see the new Newcastle and all it offers, to meet the experienced conference team, and learn about the 'special' treatment we offer, contact Vincent Sheekey, Conference Officer at the Civic Centre, or phone (0632) 610773.

8 CONFERENCE CATERING

ORACLE
BUSINESS INFORMATION

Conference Organisers
for

**Business, Financial
& General Subjects**

41 Ladbroke Grove, London, W11 3AR Telephone: 01-727 3503

---

how many glasses of wine per bottle, as drinks can quickly add many extra pounds to your bill. The price factor is not necessarily solved by bringing in your own wine, as a corkage rate is generally charged.

What service should be chosen? If delegates have been sitting for long periods of time they may enjoy a chance to stand and walk around. There may be a dinner planned for that evening, in which case a finger or fork buffet would be ideal. Should you decide on this method then do ensure that all food is in bite-sized portions, salads and meat slices should be avoided unless seating has been arranged. Keep to vol-au-vents and quiches, chicken wings and small open sandwiches, sausages on sticks or chicken livers wrapped in bacon on a stick, paté on toasted strips of bread.

Assuming that the conference packages are not acceptable, and that you are organising catering separately from the room hire, overleaf are three

117

typical menu suggestions taken from a wide range of menus offered. The menu prices are also given, but add on VAT. (Menu suggestions given by De Montfort Hotel, part of the De Vere group.)

1. Finger buffet. Price £7.25 per head
Oven fresh ham and egg pie
Hot chipolatas
Assorted sandwiches
Savoury bouchees
Chicken wings
***

Gâteau mocha
Assorted pastries
A selection of English cheeses
***

Coffee

2. Carved buffet. Price £13.50 per head (starter and sweet served at the table)
Chilled Honeydew Melon
***

Baked ham or roast beef or roast turkey or salmon *en belle vue*
served with
assorted salads and parsley potatoes
***

Fresh fruit basket
Lemon mousse
Black Forest gâteau
Cheese and biscuits
***

Coffee

3. Dinner. Price £15.75 per head
Minted avocado soup
***

Fried strips of bread-crumbed lemon sole with tartare sauce
***

Pan fried scallop of pork with paprika and lemon cream sauce

with a selection of fresh vegetables and parisienne potatoes
***
Fruit shortcake with raspberry sauce
***
Coffee

The type of conference being held more or less dictates the type of catering to be used; personal taste also plays an important part. For example, a press conference or a product launch, where people need to mix and talk, or a sales conference where ideas can be swapped, adapts well to a part-served buffet while a more formal conference dictates a waiter service. Unless you know your group very well, stay away from highly-seasoned dishes, especially if there is an afternoon session to follow.

Whatever is decided on, floral decorations can add a nice touch; and if you can persuade the caterers to have a special centrepiece, a swan carved out of ice – or possibly in the shape of your company's new product – it can often add the finishing touch. It is amazing how just a little extra thought can change an ordinary meal into a memorable event.

Entertainment and formal dinners should be kept to the end of the conference when more time is available, especially if it is planned to make a presentation or an incentive award to the best salesman. It is at these post-conference dinners that seating arrangements have to be considered very carefully. If the conference is small, under 25 delegates, try to arrange the seating plan so that everyone is on one table or if two tables are necessary, that they are placed next to each other. The conference may be a full-blown company affair with 100 or so delegates. If the restaurant is a large one, ask for it be sectioned off – alternatively a smaller room may be available. To save you time, ask each manager to look after guests seated at their table.

Presentation awards, often held after dinner, play an important role in rounding off an inter-company conference and can be seen as giving future impetus to the conference aims. But this is one decision which is not yours. The 'rewards' are organised by someone else, your role is to fit it into the conference programme. Of course, you may be asked for suggestions. The type of rewards vary from an overseas trip, a weekend for two, a case of wine, a watch, clock or some other form of annual prize giving. But there have been 'many a slip twixt cup and lip' as far as presentations are concerned with the 'popular' one being 'who has got the . . .' only to find out that the award is 100 or so miles away still languishing in the office safe. Remind whoever is responsible to bring along the award and give it to the person making the presentation.

If presentations are planned, group seatings become even more important. Tables should not be widely spread around the room so that delegates cannot hear the chairperson's remarks: try to see that tables are arranged with aisle space behind and placed so as to give unhindered viewing.

"I do hope he's going to speak English..."

When hope is not enough— break through the language barrier with simultaneous interpretation.

At international meetings, seminars and presentations, simultaneous interpretation increases comprehension by allowing delegates to speak and listen in their chosen language.

M&R provides a complete interpretation service, working with organisers from the planning stage through to the installation of the equipment and running of the system.

'Phone or write to M&R to find out how they can help your international delegates to communicate more effectively.

M & R
CONFERENCE
COMMUNICATIONS
7, Bell Industrial Estate,
50, Cunnington Street,
London W4 5HB.
Telephone: 01-995 4714/5.

8 CONFERENCE CATERING

Entertainment can also be part of the programme but do ensure that all heads of tables know beforehand where everyone is supposed to go.

Conference catering presents a challenge – that of organisation and imagination. Delegates expect good and tasty food. If the catering is poor then this reflects on their evaluation of the conference's success and on you, the conference organiser. The important thing to remember is that you do not have to spend a fortune in order to get the right balance – we all do not require caviar and champagne!

9 Planning a conference abroad

The Europeans have been organising their conferences in other countries far longer than we have. And the Americans introduced incentive travel. Only in the last 15 to 20 years have we in the British Isles seriously considered venues overseas, but now it is a growing, thriving area set to develop still further in future years.

But who organises conferences abroad, and why? And, inevitably, what is it going to cost. And yes most overseas locations will cost more, but taking into account the extra time, accommodation and catering and, of course, the airfare, it does not represent too great a price difference per head.

Overseas conferences are now more frequently held by a number of different associations and other professional bodies and the number of companies considering this route is growing. As this book is about organising a company's conference, it is useful to consider the benefits that can be gained from going to an overseas location. There are three main reasons why conferences are held overseas.

1. Location: If your company has a number of overseas subsidiaries, an equidistant location might be

9 PLANNING A CONFERENCE ABROAD

more suitable, reducing air travel of one party and placing all attendees on an equal footing.

2. Incentives: This is a growing market. Many UK companies now seek to reward their UK-based sales force by selecting an overseas location to hold their conference.

3. Location Marketing: A special marketing exercise which benefits from an out-of-the-ordinary location. A well-known example of this occurred a few years ago when a British automobile manufacturer launched its new range of cars.

A number of you might worry about organising this type of event yourself and consider whether to go to the professional sources. Remember that organising an overseas conference entails more work than a UK-based conference. For one thing, there are the airline tickets to arrange. It is a daunting task if you have not done it before. And if you do feel squeamish, and that is understandable, then by all means use a specialist (see Appendix).

As well as specialist overseas conference organisers, there are now a number of large and small travel agents who organise overseas conference trips. They have the information to hand thus saving you the time and unnecessary trouble of trying to find out what is what. A number of these firms will also have their own overseas representatives who will meet you at the airport or hotel.

But this book is not about specialist organisations, it is about doing it yourself. If you are determined to plan your firm's meeting, then allow for adequate time to organise things. Secondly, look for a suitable destination. If organising your company's UK-based meeting, allow yourself a lead time of at least six months, but for an overseas conference allow double that time. Many people have been overseas and are able to suggest a few places themselves; it is a good idea, however, to ask senior staff if they have any preference as to the destination (they may have been on an overseas conference before and be able to recommend a suitable place). Stress that you are only asking for suggestions and that the most exotic of the recommended locations may not necessarily be the one chosen. After all the site must motivate the delegates *and* the executives, who may have vested interests.

Southern Europe is the most popular area: the Spanish and Greek islands being the most popular. Other locations to consider include Italy (Venice and Rome are delightful cities), Crete and Tunisia (very good standard of hotels). Why not consider Germany (the Black Forest) and if weekend trips are preferred, consider Paris, Amsterdam and Madrid. But you need not go that far afield, Guernsey and Jersey are much closer. Both these islands have special conference centres and many good hotels to choose from. A telephone call to the Guernsey or Jersey Tourist Board will produce a comprehensive package of literature on all necessary services. Decide what you want: sun, sea and sand or capital cities and culture.

Having established the broad area of preference, then get in touch with the relevant tourist offices (some may be attached to their country's embassy) who will be able to send you details on their country. Do not forget national airlines either, Olympic are extremely helpful about all matters Greek. Explain to them what you are hoping to do and ask for recommendations as to suitable locations, and the addresses of hotels in those areas. As an overseas conference lasts for three or perhaps four days, entertainment and sightseeing trips should also be investigated. Write to these hotels requesting details as to their rates, facilities, proximity to airports, availability, etc. Local travel agents will also be able to help you on hotel reservations.

Ask the airlines, as well as travel agents, to quote on a block booking for, say, three different locations, travelling in, say, September 1987. (British Airways class 'groups' as *ten* or more people – depending on the route, airlines may offer a 'group discount', so do not forget to ask.) This will give an idea of the airfares' cost but as you will not be travelling right away, ask

9 PLANNING A CONFERENCE ABROAD

them how long the prices will be valid. If your company uses a travel agent then ask for his help in organising travel and accommodation arrangements. If your company does not use a travel agent, but you wish to on this occasion, then contact either the Association of British Travel Agents (55–57 Newman Street, London W1P 4AH) on 01-637 2444 or the Guild of Business Travel Agents (23 East Castle Street, London W1) on 01-636 1997, and ask them for the names and addresses of members in your area. A useful title to read on the subject of booking air travel is *A Consumer's Guide to Air Travel* published by Telegraph Publications.

Compare all the quotations, both from the airlines and from the hotels, before making up your mind. If you have a country of preference and the costs there are higher than the others, check and make sure that facilities are similar before making up your mind. Although cost is an important factor, it is not the sole

MONADNOCK
INTERNATIONAL
Professional Conference Organisers

MARKETING • MANAGEMENT • ADMINISTRATION

International Speakers Bureau

Management Seminars

Video Production

UK / International Projects

FOR FURTHER INFORMATION CONTACT: CHRISTOPHER WHITE, DIRECTOR MONADNOCK INTERNATIONAL LTD., 2 THE CHAPEL, ROYAL VICTORIA PATRIOTIC BUILDING, FITZHUGH GROVE, TRINITY ROAD, LONDON SW18 3SX. TEL: 01-871 2546 TELEX: 299180 MONINT G

> **ᑭ PETER PEREGRINUS LIMITED**
>
> Peter Peregrinus Limited has many years experience of organising Conferences and Exhibitions.
>
> Our skilled staff can provide an efficient and flexible service covering:
>
> | | | |
> |---|---|---|
> | Administration | Printing | Social events |
> | Venue selection | Publicity | Registration |
> | Hotel rooms | Committee support | Financial Control |
>
> We specialise in scientific and academic conferences, and general exhibitions, but however complex your requirements we can offer the skills to meet them.
>
> Call Peter Peregrinus Limited on 01-240-1871
> Conference and Exhibition Services Division
> 2 Savoy Hill, London WC2R 0BP

one and overseas locations should not be decided on cost alone; instead consider the meeting's objectives, the type of people attending, and whether there are any other important factors, such as the company's overseas representatives. Also, it is important to choose a site which fits in with the 'incentive' or 'reward' planned. It is no use booking an exotic location if it means pitching sales targets too high. If using the overseas meeting as a 'reward', ensure that the equation of destination (cost) equals target set.

Now that you have decided on the final destination, how long will the conference last? This will, of course, depend on the programme or agenda. For example, if a conference programme is to last two days then the ideal length of the trip would be three or perhaps even four days. One day to travel and settle in, two days of meetings with the last day to sightsee. (The overall length of the event may be longer if it is an incentive or reward trip.)

9 PLANNING A CONFERENCE ABROAD

As more and more people travel abroad, airline and hotel costs become more competitive. Even more so in 1986 as tourist travel has been hit with one crisis after another. From a conference organiser's point of view, it means that costs can be negotiated. An idea would be to try and avoid mid-week meetings if planning overnight accommodation, this is true for both home and abroad. Usually business reservations tie up hotel rooms during the week with weekends fairly quiet – airlines tend to have more space available at that time too – the end result being that special price deals can be negotiated, especially for large block bookings. Seasons also play a very important role. Book during the height of the season to go to any of the Southern European locations and this will inevitably mean higher travel costs and less choice in preferred accommodation. But if you arrange your conference either just before the season starts or at its end, then not only will the weather be similar to the peak season, but the prices will be reduced and a greater choice of accommodation will be available. As a rough indication of price, for a three-day conference (two days working, one day resting), held out of season in Southern Europe for thirty or so delegates, the cost will be approximately £300 to £350 per delegate (including airfare, accommodation, catering, hire of conference room). For more far-flung locations, such as India, using the same example as a guide, the cost would be approximately £450 per delegate.

Overseas inspection trips are even more important than those in the UK. If organising a large conference then the accommodation and probably the airfare may be free of charge for the first trip. Even if it is not, an inspection trip is an essential part of conference organising and should *not* be passed by. A second inspection trip may also be necessary.

All rules that govern booking of UK venues apply overseas and more. Travel arrangements to and from the airport need arranging as well as any recreational arrangements. If presentation equipment is to be hired then this has also to be arranged. The language barrier may present a problem and even simple catering arrangements may be misunderstood. If this is a likelihood, then hire a resident local translator (if possible English as a mother-tongue) or maybe your company employs a person who is bilingual in this language. You will generally find that the written word is understood more than the spoken one, so send letters of confirmation (or use the telex) as much as possible to avoid confusion. If overseas contracts are entered into, then these need to be checked over by a solicitor who is familiar with that country and its law. A specialist travel agent familiar with such undertakings may be able to recommend a specialist legal adviser.

Potential problems

Health

If travelling within Europe vaccinations are not necessary, but if organising a conference further afield, such as in Africa or Asia, then do check with your company doctor or local health authority, who will be able to tell you what vaccinations are needed. Do this well in advance as some injections need to be done seven to eight weeks before departure, with a booster some three weeks or so before the actual departure date. (If your conference is a large one, why not take your company doctor with you. This is not as uncommon as you think.)

Jet-lag to these far flung locations can also present a problem. The only solution is to allow an extra day before starting the conference.

Some illnesses need never occur and can be laid firmly at the door of human excesses, too much rich food and too much of the local wine can make your attendees feel very ill. Supply a short list of sensible 'dos and don'ts'. A wise precaution is to find out where local hospitals are, and to ask the airline or embassy what the standard of medical care is (Spain, for example, has a good health service). Insure against illness and should the illness be a serious one have insurance cover for an air-ambulance home. I have

THE CEI WORLDWIDE CONVENTION CENTRES YEARBOOK 1986

The only definitive guide to international centres.

*T*he Conferences & Exhibitions International Worldwide Convention Centres Yearbook is a brand new comprehensive and authoritative guide to the major international convention and exhibition centres throughout the world.

Each entry gives at-a-glance information to provide meetings' planners with general information and key data on all of the world's most important and popular centres. There are full colour photographs of each centre, maps showing location, detailed tables of facilities and overall plans of venues. It is truly a vital work of reference to all professional and corporate meetings' organisers and professional association meetings' planners worldwide.

The book is tastefully bound in a durable glossy cover and with its useful A4 format, it offers utility, durability and style. What's more, it's FREE (except for a contribution towards postage and packing) to all bona fide association meetings' planners. Even those who do not qualify for a free copy, the Yearbook costs just US$25 or £20 Sterling, including postage and packing.

Secure your copy of this unique and important work of reference by writing to us at the address shown below — but you'll have to hurry. Demand is heavy and the limited stocks are distributed strictly on a first come first served basis.

For full details write to: Gill Jones, International Trade Publications Ltd., FREEPOST, 2 Queensway, REDHILL, Surrey RH1 1ZA. Or telephone Redhill (0737) 68611.

always found 'Murphy's law' rules – if you do not plan well enough, then you are going to wish you had.

Insurance
Add travel, accommodation, health and lost items to your insurance policy. Try to avoid having all your key personnel travelling on one flight, and always insure for loss of key personnel. The general rule is, if there is a chance of it happening then insure for it.

Nationality
Check before your trip as to the nationality of each delegate and what passport they hold. European locations should not present too much of a problem for the non-British passport holder. However, if the firm has either an Israeli or South African working for it and the conference is to be held in the Middle East or Africa, then you have got a problem. Remember also that if your company has a senior manager who is a single woman (or a woman not accompanied by her husband) then certain Middle East countries, such as Saudi Arabia, will not allow her in.

Security springs to mind at this point: as some countries' nationals may be at greater risk than our own. Recently a tongue-in-cheek article stated that the Americans were being advised to use a razor-blade and cut off the 'Stars and Stripes' from their luggage or their blazers, and in its place sew on the Mapleleaf! But on a more serious note, when selecting the conference destination do take into account the current political climate and stay well away from countries noted for security upheavals or lapses.

Equipment problems
If the venue location tells you that equipment is available there for hire, check it when you make your first inspection trip. If taking equipment from the UK to the overseas venue site, remember that voltages and all things electrical change from country to country. If you are taking out your own equipment then go along to your local Customs and Excise office and get an

9 PLANNING A CONFERENCE ABROAD

exempt certification for each item being taken. This will ensure that VAT is not paid on the return leg. (It may also be possible to reclaim VAT on some expenses incurred while in member EEC countries.) Taking equipment into a country may require import licenses so do speak to the consul or embassy and obtain all the relevant documentation – hold-ups are not only frustrating, but costly in time and money. The last thing you want is for a conference to start without the equipment. Also ask whether there are any trade embargos; one organisation ran into trouble when organising a conference in France – the organiser was taking in some matches that clearly stated their country of origin, 'Made in Japan'.

Eight to ten weeks before the start of the trip, a detailed itinerary must be sent to all delegates, including time and location of departure point, as well as:

— necessary vaccinations;
— destination and location of conference and accommodation;
— date and time of departure from the UK (carrier, airport, flight number);
— time of arrival;
— date and time of arrival to the UK on return leg of journey (carrier, airport, flight number).

You also need to tell delegates about currency restrictions: some countries have very strict currency control – Greece is a prime example. Organise currency purchase well in advance. It is always better for each individual to make his or her own arrangements. You, on the other hand, have to make arrangements for the company and take along a float to pay for incidental costs. Take some cash but also banker's drafts (credit cards are usually acceptable but this needs to be checked). Ask the hotel whether they will accept pounds sterling (most will); currency transaction charges will be added to your bill. Remind delegates to take their driving licences with them and, of course, their passport or green cards.

D-Day Although tickets can be sent special delivery, perhaps the best course of action is to appoint a member of staff (or do it yourself!) to act as courier, meeting delegates at the preselected assembly point. If possible, assemble the group the night before at a local hotel but if this is not feasible arrange an assembly *at least* three hours before departure. A large sign should be displayed above the assembly point: the airline may be able to assist you in this. Once at the assembly point, tickets can be distributed, any last minute queries answered, and the luggage checked in. A further briefing should take place, giving clear instructions as to what happens on arrival, who else is with the party, travel arrangements at the other end, conference start time, entertainment planned, etc. The group can then clear immigration and security checks together and make their way to the duty free area.

Guest speakers and dignatories need separate and special treatment. They should be met at the airport (or taken to it) and assisted at all times. A senior member of staff should be assigned to host them for the entire meeting.

If you are lucky, the flight will not be delayed due to bad weather or strikes. But should this unhappy event occur, ascertain from the airline how long the delay is likely to be. If the flight is going to be delayed for some time, speak to the airline as they usually have a VIP lounge that may be of use. However, if this is not possible, the group will need to be kept together, so assemble them in the coffee shop or lounge – avoid the bar as some in the party may have little restraint; how embarrassing if the pilot refuses to take a member of the group on board because of drunkenness and bad behaviour. When delays occur, groups often split up and people can miss flights. The prime role of a courier in this situation is to keep the group together, which is no mean task.

Getting the group back in one piece is also a feat. Again the best way is to assemble beforehand, allow

9 PLANNING A CONFERENCE ABROAD

ample time for delegates to pay for any extras they may have ordered, such as drinks, telephone calls, etc. If not then you could be lumbered with the bill or, worse still, delegates could miss the return flight. Prior arrangements with the hotel manager or his assistant can greatly reduce the chance of this happening.

One last tip when organising a meeting overseas, ask the hotel or relevant embassy if they know of any manufacturers where, say, printing supplies can be bought. Then contact the recommended companies and ask for samples and quotations. Seeing if local supplies can be obtained may save you a lot of unnecessary trouble.

10 Introducing exhibitions

No consumer title on organising conferences or meetings would be complete without a brief discussion on exhibitions, despite the fact that they are two separate entities. An exhibition stand at the right exhibition can give maximum exposure towards new business contacts and even new markets. Rarely in a conference environment will you have to deal with unions, whereas when organising an exhibition stand, this will be an important function and one that has to be dealt with diplomatically. Colleagues will also become more involved. Having noted the differences, there are a number of common facets, such as the mechanics of organisation and the utilising of equipment. What this chapter aims to do is to dispose of the saying, 'it will be all right on the night': without proper thought, planning and organisation your company's exhibition can turn out to be a disaster.

The decision whether to have an exhibition stand and where it is located is vital. What are the objectives? What is your proposed target market? Are you currently in this market or is the purpose to seek out and develop a new market? What other similar

10 INTRODUCING EXHIBITIONS

exhibitions are planned over the next year to eighteen months? Are there any subdivisions within the exhibition itself? Getting answers to these questions will show how important your appointment is. After you have gained answers, make it very clear to all staff involved precisely what the company's objectives are in relation to this exhibition.

The next step is to agree a budget. A budget layout is shown in Chapter 2. When you organise an exhibition (as opposed to a conference) there are going to be certain additions and certain deletions from the budget list shown on page 23. The notable additions will include the stand (its design and construction), product display and any promotion both before and during the exhibition, exhibition stand rent (as opposed to room hire in conferences). If comparing the same size conference to an exhibition, the staff costings will be greater as more time and effort will be needed prior to the opening of the exhibition and during the exhibition's life. Your aim must be to gain the whole-hearted commitment of the staff – and if they have helped with the organisation, reward them by taking all helpers along to the exhibition. Having trained staff who know about the company and the products is a far better management decision than leaving them behind and hiring 'dolly birds' for three or so days who know nothing about your company or product. Although it is good personnel policy to take along new members of staff to the exhibition, do not let them man the stand.

Appointing a good and experienced stand designer is the next stage. If there is no-one within your organisation who fulfills this role (as it is such a specialised function, it is unlikely that you will have such in-house expertise) then contact the British Exhibition Contractors Association (BECA) (for the address and telephone number see the Appendix). They will be able to supply a list of their members. If in doubt or in need of advice, there are a number of associations dedicated to assisting the setting up and successful running of exhibitions.

Before appointing a specialist designer ask for references, and check with his or her clients to see:

(a) if they deliver on time and;
(b) do they work within the budget constraints.

Ask to see a number of his designs; they should be attractive and eye catching but not too unusual as to seem remote. One stand had two levels with a small hospitality suite on the first floor. There was one set of stairs. These stairs were so narrow that many visitors could not go up and when up, found it difficult to come down. A stand display must look friendly, open and inviting. I was told by an expert that if a designer did not try to make the display as welcoming as possible, allowing for interest and detail, then he or she had not done their job properly. He showed photographs of what appeared to be a conventional yet appealing stand: a closer look showed many near hidden details which would attract and retain passing visitors. The stand was sited on a corner and was laid out in a similar style to an Edwardian tea room. Tea was offered free of charge, and the seating was a welcomed change for many visitors glad at the chance to sit and rest their weary feet. On the table were menu-styled brochures and behind the tea room image, product shelving and photographs were displayed. Suitably dressed waitresses served scalding hot tea – too hot to drink right away. As they waited for the tea to cool, our visitors read the brochures. After three or four minutes, stand staff came along for a chat. As the tea was so hot, and there were no more than ten tables, the staff had ample time to see everyone, converting enquiries into leads. The last photograph showed a queue building up, with visitors waiting to get on to the stand. This is just an example, but the best thing to do is to visit a number of exhibitions and see what the different stand designs are like, and which are the most successful.

The exhibition designer must be thoroughly briefed; tell him why the company is having the stand, what products are going to be displayed, the correct name of the company or the group of companies (avoid trade names: the words 'company' and 'limited' can also be discarded); whether you wish a hospitality section added to the stand and how many on-site personnel will be present. Each exhibition site will have different dimensions so inform the designer of these. Also tell him where the stand will be located, on a corner, near to the restrooms, close by the bar and restaurant facilities (it may not be necessary for a hospitality section in this instance). If your company happens to manufacture large machines that will be on display, then this 'moving miracle' will need prior planning as they need to be incorporated into the overall image. The designer will need the exact specifications, which must be exact and include width, weight, height, etc. When the design has been completed, resist the urge, unless it is absolutely necessary, to change any details as this will add to your final bill. This is the reason why the briefing, and any ideas you may have on what design is acceptable, is so crucial.

Any 'out of the ordinary' arrangements will have to be cleared first with the exhibition organisers for suitable entrance, height clearance, etc. Some exhibition centres have height constraints; the Barbican has lower ceilings compared with the National Exhibition Centre. Your display may need water, so suitable drainage would have to be specially laid on. Extra voltage is another common requirement. Check the exhibition organiser's rules and regulations so that you are familiar with them. They will also tell you what communal arrangements have been made, including safety. And if you still have doubts, ask the exhibition organiser.

When the stand design has been completed, if it is out of the ordinary, the organisers may wish to see the plans. The stand designer must abide by the rules and regulations laid down – and you must make sure that he does, if in doubt, ask the organisers. The designer may recommend a stand contractor, but throughout the organisational life of the exhibition, whatever service is contracted, do get quotations in writing and agreed well beforehand. What must be avoided are any problems on the day the exhibition opens.

Now is the time to brief your stand contractor. Make sure that he knows what items have to be collected (such as enlarged prints) and which ones will be delivered, and when. Confirm it back to him *in writing*. Keep a check on the confirmation, again make sure that there are no hidden surprises. If a machine forms a special part of your display, check it to ensure that safety guards are installed. If you feel that it could be tampered with, organise security (see page 118). A company recently exhibited a new machine, and proudly displayed it. Glowing statements were issued as to its accuracy. Unknown to the staff, during the previous evening it was tampered with. The day before crowds had gathered to see the display, and the following day people lined up again to see the machine in action. The staff invited visitors to put their watch under the machine's hydraulic press. But things went

---

Southampton Conference Marketing

THE VENUE SEARCH LINE
0703 832504

From Southampton's Guildhall to University
From theatres to stately homes
From hotels to floating venues

Tell us your specifications – we'll do the rest

THINK SOUTHAMPTON
THINK VENUE LINE 0703 832504

10 INTRODUCING EXHIBITIONS

> **Give us your next charter...**
> we'll give you
> an easy choice
> —who to use
> next time.
>
> Air conditioning available
>
> Volvo, Scania and Mercedes
> 28-53 seat
> Executive and Touring
> Coaches
>
> **THE SPECIALISTS**
>
> **Len Wright Travel**
>
> **01-568 1734**
>
> Choose your specification from
> • Double glazing • Forced air ventilation • Stereo/Radio/Cassette/PA system • Toilet/Washroom • Video system
> • Hot drinks service • Hot/Cold food • Refrigerator • Bar/Servery • Tables • Hot/Cold water • Air conditioning
> Unit 3, Fleming Way, Worton Road, Isleworth, Middlesex TW7 6EU. Telex: 892339.

wrong. The first visitor duly obliged and placed his expensive watch on the appointed spot. Seconds later the press descended, only this time it failed to stop; the customer's watch was shattered. That lapse in security caused the company loss of face, loss of a customer and an insurance claim.

Insurance cover will have to be arranged as well as transport to and from the site. Accommodation needs booking well in advance. Before finalising the transport arrangements, check that drivers, or anyone working in the physical construction of your stand, hold the right union card. Many an exhibition stand has been unnecessarily delayed as union members refuse to finish off the lighting (or some other task) because they discovered a non-union member working on the stand. You will be surprised how easily egos can be rubbed the wrong way so do proceed with caution.

If the exhibition is going to be held at a large venue, such as the National Exhibition Centre,

139

accommodation will have to be booked many months in advance, especially if all the halls are in use. Not long after the NEC opened, I met a former colleague who had tried to book accommodation a few weeks before the exhibition. All the NEC halls were in use at the time and the volume of visitors and exhibitors was at its peak. All hotels were full and he had to stay in Nottingham. Indeed, if your company is going to have an annual stand at a time when there are a number of exhibitions on, simply ask the hotel to hold the necessary rooms in advance, firming up the exact number a few months beforehand.

Keeping the exhibition stand tidy for one week can be an uphill task. Exhibition organisers arrange for general cleaning of gangways and communal areas, but not for stand cleaning. Certain other arrangements will have to be made with the organisers for any floral arrangements for the stand. Contact British Telecom in advance asking them to install a telephone on the stand. A word of warning with regard to the telephone, lock it away after-hours (and this goes for any movable equipment too) as unauthorised use of the telephone can and will take place.

Who is going to be invited to the stand? The organiser will give your company a certain amount of complementary tickets and badges, which will need careful allocation. Draw up a guest list for both UK and overseas clients. Invitations need sending out in good time along with tickets. (Badges should also be requested at this time as delays could leave staff having to pay to get in).

The company's marketing manager may decide on a pre-exhibition publicity campaign, linking in with the aim and theme of the stand. An advertisement can also be placed in the exhibition's handbook which is sold throughout the time (a free stand entry is included when you reserve floor space).

The decision as to how much literature should be on the stand is up to you and your colleagues. There are arguments both for and against having endless supplies. Whatever is decided, copies will need to be printed beforehand and delivered in plenty of time. If overseas customers have been invited then translation of any new brochures may need to be done. An interpreter may need to be hired on the day these visitors arrive. (See Appendix for addresses.)

Security

Stand security is important as the example on page 138 shows. Throughout the exhibition, clients and potential clients will be visiting and taking away literature. Your stand staff will be busy taking down new contact names and addresses; by day three, this list should be impressive, good future sales leads in the weeks to come. It is sad, but nonetheless true, that industrial espionage does take place and is growing; competitors would give 'their right arm' to get hold of your list. If the stand is under-manned, competitors have a golden opportunity to slip one of their personnel on to the stand while the other person engages the sole member of staff in conversation, and makes off with the contact file. Unbelievable though it may sound, it has happened! Names and addresses of all contacts made must be collected at the end of each day and taken away to a secure location, possibly placed in a safe at the hotel. Make the stand staff aware of industrial espionage and stress the importance of being vigilant. If security is going to be a real and possibly an expensive problem, then speak to security experts.

One large corporation found a way round this problem and by doing so overcame another. For one week, they brought in two of their secretaries along with typewriters and as soon as a visitor expressed an interest in obtaining literature, they were taken through to a specially laid out area. The visitor's name and address was typed on an envelope and brochures were despatched on that day. The bonus was the efficient manner of the operation and the visitor did not have to carry bulky literature around. Do remember, however, to take carbon copies of names and addresses.

Stand staff

Any staff manning your company's stand need careful selection and training. A one day course on presentation methods, revision of products, and the company's aims should be organised. They also need to be shown where all the exhibition facilities are located. Plan staff rosters carefully, and put one person in charge of the stand throughout the exhibition.

Train the staff as to the best way of welcoming visitors on to the stand. Training videos can be hired for a day and used as part of the company's training programme. These videos show the 'dos and don'ts' of stand manning. Video Arts Limited at 68 Oxford Street, London (01-637 7288) offer a wide range of training videos for the industry.

There is an art in manning a stand. Rush over to visitors as they appear and see how quickly they leave the stand. If staff are marshalled at all corners with their arms crossed and a bland expression on their faces, visitors will be repelled. If staff sit around smoking and drinking coffee, chatting about the night before – visitors will feel they are interrupting and will not stop. On the other hand, offer a friendly smile as the visitors come on, leaving them for a few minutes to wander round, then approach and make a suitable opening remark. Tell your staff to avoid using the question, 'Can I help you?' Instead ask, 'Do you use product y?' 'How does this compare with your current machinery?' or 'Have you seen this brochure on . . .?'

It is worth remembering that your company's competitors may also try to slip someone on to the stand to see what brochures and products are on display, so enquirying questions can be very useful. Questions with simple yes or no answers should be avoided. Always find out who your visitor is and whether he or she fits into the prime category, the decision-maker. Is the visitor the managing director or the purchasing officer? (The latter is the more important.) Is she from the UK or overseas? (If so which country or region.) What is the size of their company? You will always have time-wasters visiting the stand, but the only way to find out who has made a genuine enquiry is to ask suitable questions.

Careful planning is needed to ensure that ample staff attend the exhibition. Attention lapses after a few hours; and by the end of the day feet are sore and tempers often frayed. Do not allow for just three people to man a stand for a week. Results will be down and morale will be low.

At the end of each day the staff should be de-briefed at the hotel. Was it a good day? How many potential sales were made? Were the staff able to cope? (Especially relevant on the first day and the first half of the last day.) How many visitors did they have? What were the visitors interested in? Did the staff experience any problems? By asking, problems will not be allowed to grow.

Should staff have ordered any extras, then the order sheet should be passed to the stand manager with the price of the item noted on it. These in turn should be passed on to you for checking against invoices.

Staff should be asked to keep the stand tidy: brochures kept in place (but not too much in place that no-one wants to take them out). Drinks and cigarettes should be banned from the stand and kept strictly in the hospitality area, again this should be kept tidy at all times. At the end of each day, the staff should tidy up – the tidying up should not be left until the next day. Whoever holds the key may be late, and visitors arriving with the stand looking untidy and dirty will gain an unfavourable impression.

What sort of refreshments are suitable? It is best to stick to light refreshments, such as coffee, tea, soft drinks, perhaps bottles of wine and beer. Snacks such as peanuts and crisps could also be available. These should be bought beforehand and transported to the site at the start of the exhibition.

If alcohol is to be on the stand, then do lock it away at night. Also remind staff not to over-indulge, having a member of staff staggering around does not enhance the company's image.

Special visitors should be taken out to lunch, perhaps with sightseeing trips arranged for your special customers.

Dismantling a stand is an art, and when done by the professional, takes no time at all. But before you let them dismantle it, check to see whether display items will be needed in the near future. The rest should be carefully packed away for use again. Literature, drinks, sales contact list and any other movable objects, such as machinery, products, etc., should be taken away that night. The stand contractor may start to take down lighting, sign boards and other items within minutes (if not before) of the exhibition closing. He will want you to leave the stand as soon as possible as it may be dismantled and taken away that night.

If you thought that there were a lot of questions to ask before the exhibition, there are certainly a lot more questions to answer afterwards. Was it all worthwhile? Did it justify the expense? What sales leads were taken? Have these leads been followed up? How much company and product exposure was gained? Compile a report, noting successes as well as failures, and circulate this report to senior management. This report will be of great assistance when deciding on whether to attend future exhibitions. If the answer is that your company will attend next year's exhibition, do not forget to book now – it is never too early!

Finally, good feeling is easily generated and plays a part in future performance. Send a letter of thanks to all personnel who helped, expressing the company's and your appreciation. Tell them what a success it was, and you hope that you can call on them to assist next year.

A calendar of key dates

To use this calendar, work back from the date the exhibition is planned to start. It shows job sequence planning which needs to be co-ordinated. The exhibition organiser's duty is to fix tasks, convene meetings, follow through on decisions, inspect all

10 INTRODUCING EXHIBITIONS

tenders and check through all invoices. The chart progression assumes that the decision to have an exhibition stand has already been agreed. The table also outlines the four areas of planning production, stand design and construction, as well as the administrative work which has to be done by the organiser (column without a heading) and promotion.

No. of months to go	Production Department	Stand Design & Construction	Promotion
		1 Decision to Exhibit	Advise PR/ Advtsg Agency
−12		2 Reserve Site 3 Agree Budget	
−11	5 Agree Product Display	4 Appoint Stand Designer	
−10		8 Brief Stand Designer	
−9		9 Stand Design	
−8	6 Order & Prepare Special Exhibits	16 Approve Stand Design	
−7		17 Submit Plans to Organiser	
−6		18 Tender to Stand Contractor	34 Plan Advertising & Publicity Policy 36 Place Back-up Advtsg Overseas
−5		19 Appoint & Brief Stand Contractor 10 Order Electricity, Water & Compair	47 Prepare Press Release No. 1 35 Agree Back-up up Advtsg 42 Stand Literature, Exbtn. Tech. brochures

HOW TO SET UP AND RUN CONFERENCES AND MEETINGS

No. of months to go	Production Department	Stand Design & Construction		Promotion
		12 Order Plumbing Fitments 12 Order Stand Extras, Furniture, Flowers etc. 15 Supply Nameboard Details		40 Photographs 43 Arrange Translations
−4		20 Approve Working Details 14 Arrange Insurance 11 Arrange Stand Cleaning	22 Plan Staff Requirements 27 Invite Overseas Agents 28 Arrange Hotel Accommodation	44 Typesetting 29 Prepare Guest Lists 30 Order Tickets & Badges 41 Place Exbtn. Ad. in Exbtn. Catalogue
−3	7 Arrange Transport (Loading, cranes, fork lift & return)	21 Stand Building (Prefabrication)	23 Select Staff	31 Prepare Ticket Despatch 37 Place Back-up Advtsg. in UK 38 Despatch overseas copy 48 Prepare Press Release No. 2 32 Despatch Tickets Overseas
−2	Check print Discuss assembly with site staff/run-in machinery	Dry run at stand builders Check all print	24 Staff Training Programme 26 Arrange Staff Roster	45 Print Delivery 35 Despatch Tickets in UK 39 Despatch UK copy 49 Prepare Press Release No. 3 51 Arrange Press Reception 52 Send Out Invitations 54 Arrange Photographer 46 Complete Advtsg/Lit Plans

10 INTRODUCING EXHIBITIONS

Norwich's fourteenth century friars had some very good habits...

In 1360 the Dominican Friars (popularly known as Blackfriars), completed the construction of their convent church. St Andrews and Blackfriars Halls formed part of the original building and now, six centuries, and an immense amount of superb renovation work later, they offer a quite unique conference and exhibition venue in the centre of the fine city of Norwich.

You can confer—there's versatile seating in two halls for 400 and 900 **plus** flexible platform arrangements, a choice of syndicate, seminar and reception areas, **and** a full range of AV equipment.

You can make an exhibition of yourself—there's over 10,000 square feet of space in which to do it, with easy access and a full range of services.

You can eat how you like—from cafeteria to full silver service, from the odd cup of coffee to a lavish banquet, all complemented by licensed bars.

You can stay nearby—there's a wide selection of accommodation within close proximity.

Our habits are quite nice, too!

Just contact: Timothy Aldous, General Manager, St Andrew's Hall, St Andrew's Plain, NORWICH NR3 1AU Telephone: (0603) 628477

CITY OF NORWICH AMENITIES

No. of months to go	Production Department	Stand Design & Construction		Promotion
−1		56 Construct Stand/ Exhibition Eve	25 Brief Staff	50 Prepare Press Release No. 4 53 Final Organisation Press Reception
		58 The Exhibition		57 Hold Receptions
		59 Dismantle Stand		55 Continuing Press Releases

Source: Reproduced by courtesy of Video Arts Limited.

11 Has it been a success?

How can the success, or failure, of a conference be assessed? Before that question can be answered together with the many immediate, short and long term implications, you must establish what the objectives were in the first instance. That may appear to be stating the obvious. But it has to be acknowledged that there are many conferences and related events where the aims have not been thought through and planned with any direction or intended conclusions whatsoever. Many companies, even in the 1980s, continue to hold meetings: 'because we always have a conference at this time'. Surprisingly, there are still companies which hold meetings with few if any objectives declared in advance. Worse still, some take place with those responsible literally floundering for subjects and activities to fill in the time simply because tradition has decreed that the conference will take place, irrespective of the need of the gathering.

This extraordinary attitude is further endorsed by companies which pre-set the duration of their conferences: 'because we always allocate that amount of time'. The economics alone of such 'traditions' are quite frightening. And it has to be said that few

11 HAS IT BEEN A SUCCESS?

companies examine in any kind of depth, the needs of what is to be accomplished and in turn to relate these to the contents of the programme and the required schedule – or indeed, whether the conference needs to take place at all.

Assuming the need, and knowing the content, the next question to ask is whether the duration should be two hours, two days or two weeks – or whatever. If the need cannot be identified, it would be sensible, and logical, to postpone the meeting or cancel it altogether. But stating the obvious will not stop so many companies concluding meetings by settling a future date and duration without due regard to need. This observation has also to be tempered with the further realism that exchange of memoranda and/or telephone calls could probably eliminate the requirement for some meetings – and conversely, prove that other meetings are necessary and should be held.

The ultimate assessment of a meeting's success can be hampered by a number of factors. For example, some companies experience difficulties when it comes to deciding who should actually attend. Many employees feel they have a right to be present and they can become habitual attendees without contributing in positive terms to the conference. Alternatively, it has to be said also that some are not given the opportunity to participate, even though they would have a contributory role to play.

Assessing the success or failure of a conference is viewed ultimately from the point of view of the company, of course. If the objectives of conveying whatever theme have been adopted and achieved in an enjoyable but business-like atmosphere, then most companies will be more than satisfied with the result. As commendable as it may appear, it really requires much more attention than merely a declaration of satisfaction that the event went off without any major problems, or that all the presentations appeared to be put across effectively. This criteria alone cannot be accepted as the reason for 'success'. It would be relatively easy for you to prepare a report of the event that would appease the directors and the shareholders, before the document was filed away and forgotten in the company archives. That approach and conclusion could be quite misleading.

Any assessments must begin with reactions and the involvement of the participants. For many it is an excuse to get away from what they regard as their daily routines. The conference is a pleasant interlude where they can meet old and new colleagues. The event is for some an occasion to look forward to. When compiling your programme, boring and stale 'lectures' should have been avoided. It has to be said, too, that many executives use the platform as an ego trip with little or no consideration being given to those who are forced to listen. You may have been lucky and not come across this problem, but if you had, you would testify to the difficulty because, due to the hierarchy of most companies, it is seldom possible to tell presenters how bad they are in terms of their ability to 'perform'. Who in the company is going to have the courage to tell them and run the risk of any repercussions resulting from such advice?

Then you will face the other kind of reaction from participants, who almost live in fear of the forthcoming conference because they will have some attention focussed upon them at sometime or other during the event. For example, it could be that they have been assigned a 20 minute period to present the sales budget and forecasts for the past year and the year ahead. These figures are then to be scrutinised and discussed by all those present. Some people revel in such situations but for others it is an ordeal and will cost hours of lost sleep and days of unrest from the moment the assignment is made to the actual moment of presentation. Even those who do not expect to be in the limelight can be very apprehensive about their roles because they feel ill-equipped and therefore uncomfortable about their participation. Psychologically they feel unable to respond satisfactorily to the standards which they believe are set by their colleagues, or peers.

11 HAS IT BEEN A SUCCESS?

There are those in every level of management through to the most junior, in terms of age, experience and length of service, who prefer the comfort and security of the day-to-day environment where they feel protected. For them, too, even if their roles at the conference are merely being observers with limited or no involvement, the procedures at the conference are not going to be an enjoyable experience. Also though admittedly these are generalisations, there are some who look forward to the company conference and others who just want the event over and done with as soon as possible.

When the final assessment is made, each company selects different factors in siting whether that conference has been a success or failure. The following pages of Case Studies reveal the range of thought. A conference manager was recently asked how he judged whether the conference was a success, his reply was succinct and to the point: 'if it has been a success, they come back'.

Whatever factors you and your colleagues decide on, there is one goal which should be aimed at – be as professional as you can. If you can enjoy yourself as well then that is an added bonus.

Case Study The preparation for a national sales meeting, a sales meeting for staff of an overseas distributor, or a trade show at any number of international venues, is very similar. There are six common factors.

DATE: Fix a date (which in the case of Trade Shows is predetermined).

SPACE: Book a venue, ensuring that it is in a convenient location and offers all required services: video, catering, etc., as required in comfort (there is nothing more distracting than an uncomfortable chair or a video you cannot see or hear).

ATTENDANCE: Send a detailed invitation (as early as possible) to all those you wish to attend, showing the time and date and an indication of the purpose of the meeting.

PURPOSE: Having agreed the purpose of the meeting, work out how this can be achieved. When all areas have been covered, compile an agenda which needs to be concise but detailed.

BACK-UP: Ensure that all information necessary to aid discussion is present: figures, graphs and other literature should be given to those attending in a folder, presented in an easy-to-follow and self-explanatory format.

ON THE DAY: Having detailed an agenda, it is important to try and keep to the matter in hand. This can best be achieved by using a chairperson to control the proceedings and to minimise deviation and time-wasting.

The success of such a meeting can be assessed from the involvement and feed-back of those attending. Depending on the size of such a meeting, it can be difficult to absorb everything that is said. It is very beneficial to have one person in attendance who is not involved in the discussions, to record the relevant points covered. These observations can be circulated as minutes or a report after the meeting, to those who were present. Invariably a lot of ground is covered in a relatively short time, therefore an unbiased concise report of the proceedings is very useful to all concerned and can be studied at leisure after the event.

Depending on the original purpose of the meeting, its success can only be quantified after the event, when the 'purpose' is achieved. If the purpose was to 'sell the company', did those attending have a better understanding by the end of the meeting of the workings and objectives of the company? If the purpose was to 'launch a new product range', was the product range understood and enthusiastically received?

11 HAS IT BEEN A SUCCESS?

Although you can get an immediate impression during and after the meeting as to its success, the true success may only be assessed months later with an increased order book. Likewise with trade shows, you can have a feeling of how it went immediately after the show, but its true success may only be realised months later, when you have followed up all the leads and introductions.

Sarah Henley, PR/Sales Executive, Sari Fabrics Limited

Case Study Jaguar's conferences, business meetings and product launches are all held to achieve one fundamental objective – the communication of crucial business information with impact and memorability. Every element of conference organisation must contribute to the achievement of that objective.

At Jaguar, the approach adopted to meetings large and small, with delegates from all over the world, has proved enormously successful in achieving our communication objectives, and, more importantly, our ultimate business objectives worldwide. There are four key reasons why Jaguar's conferences have a remarkable record of success. These are:

1. Effective planning and organisation.
2. Technical systems reliability.
3. Relevance.
4. Innovation.

Those are the cornerstones of the approach which our conference and business communications company, Cricket Communications, has encouraged us to follow in a close working relationship going back over five years.

EFFECTIVE PLANNING AND ORGANISATION
Conferences and business events are notorious 'pressure points'. Directors and Senior Executives stand in the spotlight to present to internal or external audiences. The notion that 'it'll be all right on the

night' is a woefully inadequate way to manage a meeting when the credibility stakes are so high. So allow as much time as possible for the development of a conference project – even given the fast moving nature of our business. Everything is planned down to fine detail to create a map of the project to guide its development. We stay to the path we have set ourselves as closely as possible. In particular we are sticklers about deadlines. All is scheduled, and objectives must be completed by the prescribed time.

Planning does not just include scheduling. Essential aspects of the 'project map' include the detailed script for the formal sessions, the fully worked out storyboard of all on-screen visuals, the carefully considered travel and accommodation arrangements for our delegates, the design of the conference set and even the precise movement of speakers on set. This meticulous attention to detail ensures a successful, professional presentation.

The conference script – briefed by our key speakers but written in a developed conference format – is crucial, since it is the primary vehicle for the communication of our message. We believe that is a job best left to experienced professionals who can write creatively whilst still retaining the character and idiosyncracies of individual speakers.

The organisation of the conference follows the project map in a disciplined way. Internally, we identify clear areas of responsibility and allocate specific tasks to individuals. Externally, but in association with us, Cricket develop the conference through a project management team appropriate to the scale of the project. Regular integration meetings provide for progress review and feed-back.

Cricket Communication's own research has shown that the quality of hospitality provided for delegates is one of the most important factors in a successful conference. So we pay special attention to the care of our delegates – comfortable accommodation, excellent catering and relaxed, trouble-free travel arrangements.

11 HAS IT BEEN A SUCCESS?

To that end we have built a purpose designed conference theatre – one of the most sophisticated in Europe – which is equipped with state-of-the-art sound, lighting and video projection technology. This can be supplemented with hired-in systems for major conventions and launches.

Reliability is a key concern – as important with technical systems at a conference as it is in cars.

RELEVANCE

Define the objectives of any conference or business event precisely. The development of the project is then guided by the prime requirement for *relevance*. Every element of the conference must be relevant to the communication and business objectives we have set. So we disdain 'borrowed interest' – the gratuitous use of gimmicks which have no relevant bearing on the business in hand. We do use theatrical effects and spectacle but only when tightly integrated within the overall communication of our message. *Relevance* is a useful acid test when applied to any element of a conference – especially the allocation of appropriate, relevant budgets to different projects.

TECHNICAL SYSTEMS RELIABILITY

Apart from the highest quality of scripted material and the finest design of speaker support sequences and modules, the reinforcement of our Director's performance and authority at a conference demands the total *reliability* and invisibility of all the presentation technology – sound systems, lighting rig, projection facilities and theatrical effects. The aim is to create a seamless event, in which speakers and audience can concentrate without worry or distraction on the crucial objectives and content of the meeting.

INNOVATION

It is a tradition at Jaguar that we invite all our conference delegates to Coventry, to the home of Jaguar Cars.

In every other way our conferences are far from

traditional. Just as we are committed to the use of advanced, innovative technology in the cars we make, so we use innovative techniques and systems in our conferences. Recently, Jaguar staged the world's first component video conference exploiting the very latest systems to create a wholly electronic conference without a 35mm slide in sight. Equally, we have explored innovative approaches to the actual format of conferences, getting right away from speakers tied to lectern positions, allowing them to move freely about the set and develop a much closer relationship with the audience. In this way innovation ensures that our conferences and our communications have freshness and vitality.

These four fundamentals of success in conferences, presentations and business events add up to what we describe as 'the holistic approach' to conference organisation – an integrated and systematic approach which creates a whole that is so much more than the sum of the individual parts. It is certainly an approach that has contributed a great deal to Jaguar's achievement over the last few years.

Jaguar's intensive, year round programme of business conferences, presentations and conventions is rich and varied. Most are held at Jaguar's own conference centre at the company's headquarters in Coventry, England.

Peter Battam, World Marketing Services Manager, Jaguar Cars Limited

---

Case Study A trade association of manufacturing companies had held a conference every other year for 20 years. As each event approached, the additional administrative work involved was allocated by the director to those of his staff of 16, whom he considered could best handle it over and above their normal duties. Apart from the correspondence files relating to earlier conferences, no reference material was available.

One year, proposed government legislation brought

11 HAS IT BEEN A SUCCESS?

the industry into a state of potential crisis. The director decided that the coming conference should address itself exclusively to the new situation and the Government department concerned agreed to co-operate. Interest in the conference escalated, the number of registrants trebled, a hotel able to provide a larger venue was found: inevitably the inexperienced association staff, already struggling with unfamiliar work, were overwhelmed by the new organisational problems which arose.

A Professional Conference Organiser (PCO) was called in. As a first and urgent task the PCO wrote detailed schedules for the new venue, reserved extra time (fortunately available) for 'setting up'; changed the hastily agreed venue reservation to one on a 24-hour basis to avoid setting up and breaking down overnight. The PCO checked the small print of the rental conditions for such matters as loss of deposits and insurance responsibilities for damage to building fabric and public liability, and immediately recommended an all embracing abandonment and public liability insurance policy especially written at Lloyds for such conferences. The PCO then looked at the inadequate technical back-up available at the venue and recommended dual projection equipment from a trusted supplier together with a well-trained technician (whatever any hotel says, an electrician will not 'keep an eye on your projection'), and extra equipment for a proper slide preview room to be set up. Storage was investigated and found to be insecure. Speedy negotiation was started and as a result, a bedroom for this purpose was allocated by the hotel at no extra cost. Additional porterage at the precisely required time was agreed by the hotel conference manager who conceded that 'pot luck porterage' was the usual order of the day. Strong wheeled trolleys were hired for the display materials – essential for the making of the manufacturer's case against the newly proposed legislation – and two shallow ramps were added to the order to provide access.

The entire catering problem was reconsidered. The

overworked Association staff had paid little attention to the detailed arrangements and here the PCO's professionalism came into its own. The banquet menu was adjusted to avoid a repetitive diet of beef; the proffered hotel pack of assorted biscuits was discarded, Danish pastries being introduced with morning coffee and shortbread added to the tea break. Lunch was modified from a sit down, three course event to a two course fork lunch, thus spreading the energy intake more evenly and avoiding the possibility of a slumbering audience for the vital afternoon sessions.

Many other changes were suggested and finally an on-site meeting was called, drawing together for a brain-storming session on logistics the hotel conference manager, the banqueting manager, the Association's director and his staff and the front of house manager. A second briefing session was arranged for speakers, technicians, audio visual equipment providers, set designers and slide preview team, again with the hotel staff, to discuss and agree the technical arrangements.

An urgent task now for the PCO was to make the budget adjustments, to include the justifiably increased venue costs charged for bringing the facilities up to requirement; to decrease the projected per capita expense for catering with a considerable saving on the allowance for lunch; to decrease by 10 per cent the numbers given to the venue for the welcome reception and the banquet as well as for lunch (every PCO knows the considerable savings to be made for the client in the prediction of 'drop-aways'). A further look was taken at the small print on release conditions for the hotel bedrooms and the information carefully noted to avoid any forgetfulness and subsequent liability on the part of the Association. The budget was completed and agreed with the Association as a definitive document, every possible area of expenditure being fully incorporated and a 5 per cent contingency amount added as a precaution against such last minute items as

11 HAS IT BEEN A SUCCESS?

authors' corrections in the printed material, unexpected speakers' costs, or wine limits being exceeded at the various social events.

A Government minister having agreed to attend the conference, the PCO, in co-operation with the local police, made arrangements on security acceptable to the Department, and an Association officer was detailed to 'meet and greet' the dignatory on the day. A full briefing letter was despatched to the civil servants involved, asking questions such as what entourage would accompany the minister, would he attend the opening ceremony, the reception, the banquet; what background papers or biographical details could the Association be helpful with; and would press attendance be welcome or not?

With proper records, proper preparation and proper procedures but above all by giving overall responsibility to one manager who could have established and maintained a professional attitude to the tasks involved, this Association could have established a working administrative model able, without difficulty, to meet the problem of escalating numbers. Such a manager should have established a flow chart of every necessary administrative task, starting eighteen months before the conference; a budget check list of every conceivable inclusion; a venue check list including setting up and breaking down schedules; furniture and equipment lists; catering schedules; staffing timetables; briefing meeting agenda; daily memo; systems, and the list of tasks goes on.

A PCO is equipped with management expertise, well-tried procedures, and a recall able to predict every predictable difficulty leaving time to deal with the really unpredictable emergencies. The error made by this Association had been a lack of understanding of the essential professionalism required for the tasks of conference organising.

In the end the conference was a great success. The Association director now has to decide whether to appoint a full-time conference officer to his staff or to call on a PCO on a regular basis. His decision will depend on the Association's general circumstances: but he will undoubtedly have at the front of his mind the fact that engaging and following the advice of a PCO had resulted not only in an immaculately organised conference but also one which earned, through good financial management, a considerable profit for his Association's funds.

Anthea Fortescue, Managing Director, Conference Associates Limited

---

Case Study

The decision to host an international event is seldom taken lightly and often a degree of persuasion is necessary before the responsible body will consider extending the invitation. The UK Committee of the International Congress and Convention Association (ICCA) has seen this as an opportunity to research those organisations which have not met in the UK and then to win them over to the idea of holding their event here. In depth research is aided by records of the Association's previous meetings which are published by the International Congress and Convention Association's headquarters in Amsterdam. These help to establish who may be responsible for making the decision.

Once the Association and the responsible person has been pin-pointed, a meeting is arranged under the umbrella of the ICCA UK Committee to point out the advantages to the international association, the national committee and the benefit to the host country of holding the event here. Members of ICCA, representing all facets of the conference industry, are therefore able to present a complete range of services which can support and assist in the promotion of the event worldwide whilst ensuring smooth administration throughout the build-up period and during the meeting itself. This approach has proved eminently successful for there are many meetings which have taken place or will be doing so in the

11 HAS IT BEEN A SUCCESS?

future which, without this intervention, would not have met in the UK.

Each conference will have its own particular requirements. Some will require service from all facets of the industry whilst others may require only accommodation, meeting facilities and perhaps a professional conference organiser. Equally, the bidding procedures have to be tailored to the character of the particular event. For instance, the ICCA announcement of the 1983 meeting of the European section of the International Association of Gerontology in Budapest revealed that this event had not been held in the UK. Approaches were made to the appropriate British societies, and as a result a bid was presented during the Budapest meeting, sponsored by the British Tourist Authority, The Brighton Centre and a professional conference organiser. This bid was accepted and the event will now take place in Brighton from the 16th to the 18th September 1987. There will be an anticipated attendance of 1,200, of which 900 will be overseas delegates. Up to 300 accompanying persons are expected.

Promotion of the event will involve ICCA members throughout the worldwide network who will offer their services to individual groups of delegates travelling to Brighton for this meeting.

Fred Wakefield, President, International Congress and Covention Association

Case Study

According to four recent organisers who based their conference at the University of Newcastle, there are four categories that they used to measure their own individual successes: organisation, financial, social and scientific/professional.

A successfully organised conference requires the smallest possible committee of people charged with making the appropriate arrangements. These people must liaise within clearly defined objectives with single identifiable members of the venue. Not only must the venue be appropriate, but there must be a lot of interaction between the venue and the organiser. Both parties need to be keen, efficient and imaginative. The most effective organising committee has but one member.

Financial success means that organisers lose no money and if possible, or where appropriate, must make a profit which is used to float another paying event. On this basis, detailed costings have to be generated from the start and it has to be assumed that all costs are met from registration fees in the case of a fee-paying seminar. Since most organisations will attempt to raise support from commercial and other bodies, this means that any money thus generated will cover the cost of unexpected incidentals and will act as a contingency reserve. Basic accommodation charges should include an overhead charge to cover the costs of the organising body. A realistic overhead might be 15 per cent.

One problem in using a university can be that halls of residence tend to be large, basic units which function well for large numbers of people but offer few of the luxuries of major hotels. This is obviously reflected in the value for money prices offered by universities. It is therefore important to ensure that there is a reasonably active social life for participants and that participants form a coherent unit within the accommodation available. Such a social programme requires imagination from the organiser and venue alike and often a large degree of flexibility from the venue alone.

Scientific and professional successes depend very much on the quality of the material to be presented. The accommodation and back-up services must work in unison. Speakers must be audible, slides must be visible and delegates must enjoy these in comfortable surroundings. Furthermore, back-up facilities should always be available. It is disastrous if a projector lamp blows and there is no back-up projector. The provision of a spare bulb is unlikely to be as helpful as a back-up projector, particularly if one has to wait for

11 HAS IT BEEN A SUCCESS?

the blown lamp to cool before it can be extracted.

In many respects, the venue uses the same yardstick for measuring success as the organiser. The prime concern must be for overall success of the event even if that means recommending that a particular aspect of the conference uses a competitor. At the end of the day the University of Newcastle wants to hear that the event was a success in Newcastle. Participants will forgive many minor problems, as there will inevitably be with large groups, if these participants are treated with courtesy, understanding and good humour by the employees and management of the venue.

Everyone should remember the 'Newcastle Conference' as a success. As a result, we feel that all the hard work was worthwhile and look back with pleasure and satisfaction at the excellent co-operation with all those involved.

Andrew Williamson, Conference Manager, University of Newcastle upon Tyne

---

Case Study

- Choose a venue which is easily accessible to intending delegates.
- Choose a subject/subjects which delegates are anxious to increase their knowledge of, and provide additional opportunities for them to meet for social discussion on the subjects during the course of the conference.
- Choose a chairperson who is both knowledgeable and firm, and who keeps speakers to time not allowing any one individual to hold the floor too long in discussions.

A good convenor is essential for technical conferences such as ours, contributing towards assembling a balanced programme, liaising with prospective speakers and refereeing the technical papers, which will be presented at the conference.

Venue and facilities must have good acoustics, adequate ventilation and air conditioning if necessary. Comfortable seating is most important. Adequate PA and AV equipment is necessary and must be efficiently operated and controlled.

Catering and refreshments need not be elaborate but must be served efficiently. Queueing either at bars or for coffee/tea should be avoided if at all possible. If delegates are to be seated, then service must be rapid and quiet, especially if there are to be toasts and speeches. For a buffet, the facilities must be adequate for all delegates to serve themselves with ease.

Good co-ordination and liaison is vital, within the organisation team and with outside bodies. Maintaining a good working relationship with the people who are providing the services is most important.

Attention to detail and special requests is important, for example, vegetarian meals, special seating, conveying messages and telephone calls, taxi services, etc. Have as much information to hand about local transport arrangements as possible. And have as many office aids available as possible – even pins and paper clips.

If you have put enough into the organisation beforehand, your calm and relaxed attitude will communicate to the meeting as a whole.

Judy Whittan, Conference Organiser, The Institution of Agricultural Engineers

---

Case Study Our annual sales conference has three main purposes:
1. To inform and inspire our sales representatives about new books to be published over the next 12 months.
2. To provide a forum in which the field sales people can feed back useful market information to the editors and help to develop new ideas.
3. To help to foster a sense of belonging and boost morale.

One of the main difficulties we experience is in trying to make some of the more technical books Kogan Page publish sound like interesting and

11 HAS IT BEEN A SUCCESS?

exciting ones. For example, there is not a lot that can be said about Ring Complex Granites and Anorogenic Magmatism which is of compelling interest to anyone other than a mineralogist engaged in research into this particular subject. To rise to this challenge is, I believe, an extremely beneficial exercise for any editor, who must address such key questions as: Who will buy this book? How are we going to reach the end user? Why should a book shop stock this book?

Clearly, even with the best and most persuasive and articulate editors, the audience's attention span is limited to about an hour at a time when it comes to absorbing highly abstract and technical information. We therefore try to intersperse sessions on our technical books with short discussions on marketing and promotion, alternating between technical books and our more accessible general titles. Wherever possible, we try to use visual aids although this can prove excessively time-consuming and expensive when trying to get through a programme of some 150 book titles, many of which are little more than a gleam in the author's eye at this stage.

In planning the conference, the key factors are pace and variety. This comes down to briefing the speakers carefully and giving sufficient thought to the order in which they speak, bearing in mind the likely effect they will have on the audience. The venue is also very important both in terms of comfort and facilities and also, perhaps more importantly, in terms of how well the participants feel they are being treated and the effect this has on the way they perceive the company. Accurate timing of coffee/tea breaks and the time taken to serve lunch are equally important ingredients in helping to maintain the pace and variety of the day's activities.

If there are no questions, either during the proceedings or at specially designated question times, it does *not* mean that all questions have been answered before they were asked. It is a very bad sign and means that participants have not been stimulated and have no wish to prolong the agony.

If, at the end of the conference, the participants come away with at least three new solutions to old problems, or new ideas to develop and feel they have had a good work out, then the conference has been a success. To leave a conference with copious notes and detailed product information but no burning desire to do something new or to do something better is to call the conference, at best, a very limited success.

Tom Davy, Sales Director, Kogan Page Limited

Despite the fact that conference planning requires detail and precision, once you have systematically and thoroughly organised each detail, your conference should go smoothly. There will always be slight problems, but if the event goes smoothly, then you deserve a pat on the back. However, will you remember all the details of organising your conference in, say, a year or two? Have you thought of writing a report for reference when organising future events?

Very few companies retain records of their conference, for example, why was a particular venue selected? What was the programme content? Are there any lessons to be learned? This lack of documented information is surprising because of the invaluable record it presents when preparing for future events. You may be promoted or move on to another job in another company, and the future conference organiser may not have been employed by your business at the time the last conference was held. It will save a lot of their time and expense to simply read a file rather than start the whole exercise again.

A check list of requirements provides the simple answer to this need. Check lists have been provided throughout this book and these can be used in forming documents for future reference. Any notes made can be added. From these records a profile of the event (assuming it to be similar, of course) can be created – a valuable asset for future reference.

11 HAS IT BEEN A SUCCESS?

Post script – training courses
Hopefully your company will start to hold conferences or meetings on a regular basis, and if this is the case then you may be considering the necessity to go on a training course. After all, organising a conference or meeting is a specialist skill. This need was summed up in a statement from ACE International: 'Organising a successful meeting is not something that any executive can do in his spare time. There are a million pitfalls for the unwary, and when you slip up in this business you tend to do so publicly.'

Three associations run training courses, the Association of Conference Executives (ACE International), International Association of Professional Conference Organisers (IAPCO) and the British Association of Conference Towns (BACT). Although the courses differ, all provide basic essential training. BACT has been organising training courses for many years; the length of each course varies from one day to five days. More recently, ACE International has started to run its own training course, which lasts for five days. The IAPCO training seminar is held annually in Switzerland, and provides an intensive training course for PCOs. Addresses of these organisations are given in Appendix III, and information can be obtained from them.

Appendix I

A selection of conference venue sites

The list below represents only a few possible venue sites; it is set out to give addresses of various sites throughout the UK.

Albany Hotel,
Smallbrook Queensway,
Birmingham B5 4EW
021-643 8171
Telex: 337031

Anchor Hotels Central Reservations,
4 Farnborough Road,
Farnborough,
Hampshire
0252-517517
Telex: 858875

Armathwaite Hall Hotel Limited,
Bassenthwaite Lake,
Keswick CA12 4RE
059-681 551

Atlantic Tower Thistle Hotel,
Chapel Street,
Liverpool L3 9RE
051-227 4444
Telex: 627070

Barbican Centre,
Barbican,
London EC2Y 8DS
01-638 4141

Bedford Hotel,
Kings Road,
Brighton BN1 2JF
0273-29744
Telex: 877245

Berystede Hotel,
Bagshot Road,
Sunninghill,
Ascot SL5 9JH
0990-2311

Birmingham Metropole Hotel,
National Exhibition Centre,
Birmingham B40 1NT
021-780 4242
Telex: 336129

APPENDIX I

Bournemouth Moat House Hotel,
Kynveton Road,
Bournemouth,
Dorset
0202-293311
Telex: 47186

Bowden Hotel,
Langham Road,
Bowdon,
Altrincham WA14 2HT
061-928 7121
Telex: 668208

Bromley Court Hotel,
Bromley Hill,
Bromley,
Kent
01-464 5011
Telex: 896310

Broome Park Golf & Country Club Limited,
The Broome Park Estate,
Barham, Nr. Canterbury,
Kent
0227-831701
Telex: 965516

Cairn Hotel,
Ripon Road,
Harrogate HG1 2MU
0423-504005
Telex: 57992

The Caledonian Hotel,
Princes Street,
Edinburgh EH1 2AB
031-225 2433
Telex: 72179

Cambridge Moat House,
Bar Hill,
Cambridge CB3 8EN
0954-80555
Telex: 817141

The Carlton Hotel,
East Overcliff,
Bournemouth BH1 3DN
0202-22011
Telex: 41244

Carlyon Bay Hotel,
Sea Road,
Carlyon Bay,
St Austell PL25 3RD
072681-2304
Telex: 42551

Cavendish Hotel,
Grand Parade,
Eastbourne BN21 4DH
0323-27401
Telex: 87579

Château Impney Hotel,
Droitwich Spa,
Worcestershire WR9 0BN
0905-774411
Telex: 336673

Chewton Glen Hotel,
New Milton,
Hampshire BH25 6QS
04252-5341
Telex: 41456

City Conference Centre,
76 Mark Lane,
London EC3R 7JN
01-481 8493
Telex: 886841

Country House Hotels Limited,
Burnham Beeches Hotel,
Grove Road,
Burnham S4 8DP
06286-3333

The County Hotel,
High Street,
Canterbury CT1 2RX
0227-66266
Telex: 965076

Crown Hotel,
Wetheral,
Carlisle,
Cumbria
0228-61888
Telex: 64175

HOW TO SET UP AND RUN CONFERENCES AND MEETINGS

Cumbria Grand Hotel,
Lindale Road,
Grange Over Sands LA11 6EN
0448-2331

De Montfort Hotel,
The Square,
Kenilworth CV8 1ED
0926-55944
Telex: 311012

Dormy Hotel,
New Road,
Ferndown BH22 8ES
0202-872121
Telex: 418301

The Dunkenhalgh Hotel,
Blackburn Road,
Clayton-le-Moors,
Accrington BB5 5JP
0254-398021
Telex: 63282

The Egerton House Hotel,
Blackburn Road,
Egerton,
Bolton,
Lancashire
0204-57171

Elstree Moat House,
Barnet by pass,
Borehamwood WD6 5PU
01-953 1622

Excelsior Hotel London-Heathrow,
Bath Road,
West Drayton UB7 0BU
01-759 6611
Telex: 24525

Fort Regent Conference Centre,
St Helier,
Jersey,
Channel Islands
0534-73000

The Garden House Hotel,
Granta Place,
Mill Lane,
Cambridge CB2 1RT
0223-63421
Telex: 81463

Gleneagles Hotel,
Auchterarder,
Perthshire PH3 1NF
07646-2231
Telex: 76105

Golden Valley Thistle Hotel,
Gloucester Road,
Cheltenham GL51 0TS
0242-32691
Telex: 43410

Grand Hotel,
Broad Street,
Bristol BS1 2EL
0272-291645
Telex: 449889

Highgate House Conference Centre,
Creaton,
Nr Northampton NN6 8NN
060-124 461
Telex: 31438

Hilton International Kensington,
179–99 Holland Park Avenue,
London W11 4UL
01-603 3355
Telex: 919763

Hotel de la Bere & Country Club,
Southam,
Cheltenham GL52 3NH
0242-37771
Telex: 43332

Hotel Leofric,
Broadgate,
Coventry CV1 1LZ
0203-21371
Telex: 311193

APPENDIX I

Institute of Directors,
116 Pall Mall,
London SW1Y 5ED
01-839 1233
Telex: 21614

Ladbroke Crown & Mitre Hotel,
English Street,
Carlisle CA3 8HZ
0228-25491
Telex: 64183

Ladbroke International Hotel,
New Street,
Birmingham B2 4RX
021-643 2747
Telex: 338331

Lane End Conference Centre,
Church Road,
Lane End,
Nr High Wycombe,
Buckinghamshire
0494-881685
Telex: 83347

The Last Drop Village,
Bromley Cross,
Bolton,
Lancashire
0204-591131
Telex: 635322

Leeds Castle Enterprises Limited,
Leeds Castle,
Maidstone ME17 1PL
0622-65400
Telex: 965737

Lydiard Park Conference Centre,
Lydiard Tregoze,
Swindon,
Wiltshire
0494-881685
Telex: 83347

Majestic,
Ripon Road,
Harrogate HG1 2MU
0423-68972
Telex: 57918

Norfolk Hotel,
Harrington Road,
London SW7 3ER
01-589 8191
Telex: 23241

North British Hotel,
Princes Street,
Edinburgh EH2 2EQ
031-556 2414
Telex: 72332

Oatlands Park Hotel,
Oatlands Drive,
Weybridge KT13 9HB
0932-47242
Telex: 915123

Old Course Golf and Country Club,
Old Station Road,
St Andrews KY16 9SP
0334-74371
Telex: 76280

Palace Hotel,
Palace Road,
Buxton,
Derbyshire
0298-2001

Pale Hall Hotel,
Llandderfel,
Bala,
Gwynedd LL23 7PS
0678-3285

Park Hall Leisure plc,
Charnock Richard,
Chorley PR7 5LP
0257-452090
Telex: 677604

Pembroke Hotel,
North Promenade,
Blackpool FY1 2JQ
0253-23434
Telex: 677469

HOW TO SET UP AND RUN CONFERENCES AND MEETINGS

Penns Hall Hotel,
Penns Lane,
Sutton Coldfield B76 8LH
021-351 3111
Telex: 335789

Queen Elizabeth II Conference Centre,
Broad Sanctuary,
London SW1P 3EE
01-222 5000
Telex: 6226699

Queen's Hotel,
Marine Parade,
Eastbourne BN21 3DY
0323-22822
Telex: 877736

Runnymede Hotel,
Windsor Road,
Egham TW20 0AG
0784-36171
Telex: 934900

Selsdon Park Hotel,
Sanderstead,
South Croydon CR2 8YA
01-657 8811
Telex: 945003

South Marston Hotel & Country Club,
South Marston,
Swindon,
Wiltshire
0793-827777
Telex: 444634

Springfield Country Hotel,
Grange Road,
Stoborough,
Wareham,
Dorset
09295-2177/51785

St Brides Hotel,
Saundersfoot,
Dyfed SA69 9NH
0834-812304
Telex: 48350

St John's Swallow Hotel,
651 Warwick Road,
Solihull B91 1AT
021-705 6777
Telex: 339352

St Pierre Park Hotel Limited,
Rohais,
St Peter Port,
Guernsey,
Channel Islands
0481-28282
Telex: 4191662

Strathallan Thistle Hotel,
225 Hagley Road,
Edgbaston,
Birmingham B16 9RY
021-455 9777
Telex: 336680

Swan House Special Events Limited,
Holly Road,
Hampton Hill TW12 1PZ
01-783 0055

Telford Hotel Golf and Country Club,
Great Hay,
Sutton Hill,
Telford TF7 4DT
0952-585642
Telex: 35481

Tickled Trout Hotel,
Preston New Road,
Samlesbury,
Preston,
Lancashire
077-477 671
Telex: 677625

Unicorn Hotel,
Prince Street,
Bristol BS1 4QF
0272-294811
Telex: 44315

University Arms Hotel,
Regent Street,
Cambridge CB2 1AD
0223-351241
Telex: 877311

APPENDIX I

University of London,
(Bloomsbury Conference Agency),
15 Woburn Square,
London WC1H 0NS
01-636 8000
Telex: 269400

University of Newcastle Upon Tyne,
3 Park Terrace,
Newcastle Upon Tyne NE1 7RU
091-232 8511
Telex: 53654

Watershed Conference Facility,
Canons Road,
Bristol BS1 5TX
0272-276444

Wembley Conference Centre,
Empire Way,
Wembley HA9 0DW
01-902 8833
Telex: 8811735

Appendix II

Other useful addresses

The list below is not a definitive list, it represents only a brief selection from conference and exhibition organisers to conference travel organisers.

Conference and exhibition organisers

Campaign Services,
Kelsey House,
High Street,
Beckenham BR3 1AN
01-658 0131
Telex: 896827

C.M.A. Limited,
Delta House,
Cornet Street,
St Peter Port,
Guernsey,
Channel Islands
0481-28007

Concorde Services Limited,
10 Wendell Road,
London W12 9RT
01-743 3106
Telex: 946240

Conexion,
72 Fielding Road,
Bedford Park,
Chiswick,
London W4 1DB
01-995 8356
Telex: 8956130

Conference Associates Limited,
27a Medway Street,
London SW1P 2BD
01-222 9493
Telex: 934346

GHC (Conference & Exhibitions) Limited,
223 Ingram Street,
Glasgow G1 1DA
041-248 2428
Telex: 777059

Eximio,
17 Shirley Gardens,
London W7 3PT
01-579 2944
Telex: 8954102

Expo Productions Limited,
222 Inverson Road,
London NW6 2HN
01-372 5636
Telex: 28569

Forman Communications Limited,
Conference Division,
Hulton House,
161–6 Fleet Street,
London EC4A 2DP
01-353 7781
Telex: 883295

George Newson Exhibitions,
P O Box 68,
Ipswich IP6 9RY
0473-210136

Meetings World Limited,
P O Box 893,
London W6 8PG
01-629 4917

APPENDIX II

The Moorgate Group plc,
Moorgate House,
56–8 Artillery Lane,
London E1 7LS
01-377 2400

Protocol Conference Management Services Limited,
5 Ching Court,
15 Shelton Street,
London WC2H 9DG
01-240 5815
Telex: 266419

Caroline Roney,
(Medical Conference Organiser),
100 Park Road,
London NW1 4RN
01-723 6722

Conference Travel
Compass Travel,
46 Albemarle Street,
London W1X 4EP
01-408 4343
Telex: 296006

Hogg Robinson (Travel) Limited,
16 Bishops Court,
Off Old Bailey,
London EC4M 7BL
01-248 1559
Telex: 269408

LEP International Meetings Organisers,
20 Dudley Road,
Tunbridge Wells TN1 1LF
0892-42011

Multitours – Conference & Incentive Division,
21 Sussex Street,
London SW1V 4RR
01-821 7000

Pickfords Business Tours,
Special Projects Department,
5 Friar Street,
Carter Lane,
London EC4V 5DT
01-248 9100

Conference security
Securicor Limited,
P O Box 23,
Vigilant House,
24–30 Gillingham Street,
London SW1V 1HZ
01-828 5611

Conference equipment hire – audio visual
Istead-PKH,
58 Hylton Street,
Hockley,
Birmingham B18 6HN
021-551 7871

Midland Audio-Visual,
(rear of) 186–210 New Road,
Rubery,
Birmingham B45 9JA
021-453 3141/6010

Conference TV prompting
Q-TV Prompting Services Limited,
10–20 Shorts Gardens,
London WC2
01-379 7352

Conference, translators & interpreters
Conference Interpreters Group,
10 Barley Mow Passage,
London W4 4PH
01-995 0801

Interlingua Language Services,
Ashurst Wood,
East Grinstead,
Sussex RH1 3RX
034-282 2101

Conference venue bookings
Expotel Hotel Reservations Limited,
Banda House,
Cambridge Grove,
Hammersmith,
London W6 0LE
01-568 8765
Telex: 8811951

Appendix III

Associations

Association of British Chambers of Commerce,
Sovereign House,
212a Shaftesbury Avenue,
London WC2H 8EW
01-240 5831

Association of British Professional Conference Organisers (ABPCO),
c/o Conference Associates,
27a Medway Street,
London SW1 2BD
01-222 9493

Association of British Travel Agents (ABTA),
55–57 Newman Street,
London W1P 4AH
01-637 2444

Association of Conference Executives (ACE International),
Riverside House,
High Street,
Huntingdon PE18 6SE
0480-5759516

Association of Exhibition Organisers Limited (AEO),
9 Totteridge Avenue,
High Wycombe HP13 6XG
0494-30430

Association of Hotel Booking Agents,
Globegate House,
Pound Lane,
London NW10 2LB
01-459 1212

Association of Official Shorthand Writers Limited,
2 New Square,
London WC2
01-405 9884

Association of Sound and Communications Engineers Limited,
4b High Street,
Burnham,
Slough SL1 7JH
06286-67633

Audio Visual and Presentation Advisory Service (AVPAS),
P O Box 21,
10–12 Fore Street,
Trowbridge BA14 8UB
02214-68083

British Association of Conference Towns (BACT),
International House,
36 Dudley Road,
Royal Tunbridge Wells TN1 1LB
0892-33442

British Association of Hotel Representatives (BAHREP),
Banda House,
Cambridge Grove,
London W6 0LE
01-741 4301

British Conference and Exhibition Centres Export Council,
c/o British Tourist Authority,
239 Old Marylebone Road,
London NW1 5QT
01-262 0141

British Exhibition Contractors Association (BECA),
Kingsmere House,
Graham Road,
Wimbledon,
London SW19 3SR
01-543 3888

APPENDIX III

British Exhibition Venues Association,
International House,
36 Dudley Road,
Royal Tunbridge Wells TN1 1LB
0892-33442

British Universities Accommodation Consortium Limited
(BUAC),
P O Box 204,
University Park,
Nottingham NG7 2RD
0602-504571

Conference Managers Association,
c/o Schwarzkopf Limited,
Penn Road,
Aylesbury HP21 8HL
0296-88101

Guild of British Travel Agents,
c/o Cadogan Travel Limited,
Cadogan House,
9–10 Portland Street,
Southampton SO9 1ZP
0703-332551

Hotel Industry Marketing Group (HIMG),
c/o Leading Hotels of the World,
15 New Bridge Street,
London EC4V 6AU
01-583 4211

Institute of Sales Promotion,
Panstar House,
13–15 Swakeleys Road,
Ickenham,
Middlesex
089-56 74281

International Association of Professional Conference Organisers
(IAPCO),
40 Rue Washington,
1050 Brussels,
Belgium,
332-640 1808

International Congress and Convention Association (ICCA),
International House,
36 Dudley Road,
Royal Tunbridge Wells TV1 1LB
0892-42011

National Association of Exhibitors (NAE),
2 Pelham Road,
South Woodford,
London E18 1PX
01-366 1291

National Joint Council for the Exhibition Industry,
UCATT House,
177 Abbeville Road,
London SW4 9RL
01-662 2442

Provisional Exhibition Centres Limited,
2 Canon's Road,
Bristol BS1 5UH
0272-298630

Scottish Conference Association,
Business Travel Department,
Scottish Tourist Board,
23 Ravelston Terrace,
Edinburgh EH4 3EW
031-332 2433

Simultaneous Interpretation Equipment Suppliers Association,
9 Hespers Mews,
London SW5 0HH
01-373 9474

Index

accommodation, 42, 46, 47, 82, 103, 139, 140
ACEPLAN, 104
agenda, 30, 126, 152
airlines, 124
 tickets, 123
assistance,
 administrative, 104–105
 conference staff, 109
 exhibition staff, 142–143
 secretarial, 104–105
Association of British Travel Agents, 125
Association of Conference Executives (ACE International), 55, 104, 167
audience, 2, 30, 31, 70, 156
 holding interest of, 81–94
 levels of concentration, 3, 165
 retention, 89
 target, 62
audio visual (AV),
 as a benefit, 61–62
 as an aid, 59–60
 choosing, 56–80
 directing, 65
 facts and figures, 75
 hire vs purchase, 68–69
 making a programme, 64–68
 narration, 66
 photography, 66
 rules, 66
 use of, 73–75
Audio Visual Presentation Advisory Service (AVPAS), 78

Badges, 102, 140
bought ledger sheet, 27
British Airways,
 group travel, 124
British Association of Conference Towns (BACT), 55, 167
British Tourist Authority, 161
budget, 2, 4, 19–29
 adjustments, 158
 and exhibitions, 135

calendar
 for a conference, 97–100
 for an exhibition, 144–147
cash flow forecasts, 20, 26
catering, 112–121, 157–158, 164
 after-conference dinners, 115, 118
 buffet, 116, 117, 118
 decorations for table, 119
 for special diet, 115, 164
 waiter service, 116, 119
celebrities, see guest speakers
central audio mixing system, 70
chairperson, 34, 82, 88, 93, 95, 96, 120
cinemas, 41
colleges, 41–42
communication,
 and service, 108
 forms of, 47
competition, 37
conference,
 abroad, 122–133
 assessment of success, 148–167
 courier, 132
 planning, 1–6, 14–19, 95–111, 153–155
 staff, 104–105, 109
 travel costs, 127
The Conference Blue Book, 45
conference committee, 12
The Conference Green Book, 45
conference room,
 layout of, 107
 message point, 107
 registration point, 106–107, 113
 seating, 70, 107
 ventilation, 46, 107
A Consumer's Guide to Air Travel, 125
content, 2, 6, 18, 43
 technical, 42
 verbal, 3, 4
 visual, 3, 4
costs,
 fixed, 20
 overdraft, 24, 25
 variable, 20
courier, 132
currency restrictions, 131
Customs and Excise, 130

diagrams, 87–88
direct mail firms, 31
discipline factors, 60–61

economic climate
 effect of, 37, 40
educational seminars, 8
'8 hour day rate', 113, 114
entertainment, 56, 119, 121
 banquet, 38
 competition, 37
 leisure facilities, 36
 theme parties, 37
equipment,
 and overseas, 130–131
 hire of, 105–106
 replacement, 80
 spare, 109, 157
exempt certificate, 131
exhibition, 134–147
 advertisement, 140
 budget, 135
 centres, 41
 literature, 140
 stand, 140, 143

film, 9, 56, 74, 77, 87, 90
 sound film, 78
flip charts, 6, 9, 56, 90

graphs, 87–88
Guernsey Tourist Board, 124
guest speakers, *see* speakers
Guild of Business Travel Agents, 125

health, 128–130
'holistic approach', 156

incentive, 2, 31–32, 123, 126
 travel, 122
incentive conventions, 10–12
industrial espionage, 109, 141
Industrial Theatre, 41, 74
inflation, 24–25
inspection trips, *see* venue: site visits
insurance, 103–104, 129, 130, 157
 for exhibitions, 139
interpretation, 105, 141
invitations, 7, 10, 31, 32, 151
 to exhibitions, 140
itinerary, 131

Jersey Tourist Board, 124

Kodak Carousel slide tray, 76

lectern amplifier, 70
lens, 77
Letraset, 87
lighting, 106
 multi-scene, 70
list brokers, 31
literature,
 conference papers, 111
 for exhibitions, 140
 handouts, 101
 pre-conference, 100
 supporting, 9
location marketing, 123

multivision, 73–74

nationality, 130
noise levels, 108
 effect of, 47–48

objectives, 1–18, 30, 33, 62, 63, 82, 126, 153, 155
overseas conference, 12

photographs, 109
presentation,
 A/V, 88
 display, 39, 91, 102–103
 environment, 69
 literature, 101
 methods of, 89–92
presentation awards, 119, 120
presentation room, 69–72

number of people in, 76–77
technology, 155
press
 dealing with, 110
 release, 10
press conference, 9–10, 33
 catering for, 119
prize draw, 32
platform,
 type of, 89
product launch, 3, 38, 41, 92
 catering for, 119
Professional Conference Organiser, (PCO), 12, 18, 22, 38, 75, 157–160
programme, 30–39, 82, 112, 120, 127, 150
 aims of, 88–89
 breaks in, 46
 making an AV, 64–68
projectors,
 back, 70–72, 90
 fuse, 80
 overhead, 6, 9, 90
 'projection wall' for, 72
 room for, 70
 slide, 74
 video, 74
 with remote control, 87
promotional meetings, 7
public speaking, 81

quotations, 22, 25–26, 27, 125

refreshment
 breaks, 114, 115, 165
 for exhibitions, 143
rehearsal, 39, 88, 90, 91, 93
report, 166

sales meetings, 3, 6–7
 catering for, 119
screen, 77
 type of lens for, 77
script,
 changes, 93
 organising a, 63
 writing a, 65–66
seating,
 arrangements, 107
 for dinner, 120
 style of, 70
security, 108–109, 138, 139, 141, 159
Simultaneous Interpretation Equipment Suppliers Association, 105
site visit, *see* venue
slides, 56, 73, 76, 77, 87, 90, 107
 35mm, 6, 75, 76, 77

OHP transparency, 76, 79
 trays, 76
solicitor, 128
sound,
 reinforcement system, 49
 studio, 66–68
speakers, 4, 32, 34, 38, 81, 88
 allocation of time, 91
 briefing, 91, 165
 choosing, 81, 92–94
 expenses, 92
 physical movement of, 85, 90
 prospective, 30
 treatment of, 132
 voice, 90
speech,
 delivery of, 86, 87
 planning, 84, 85–89
stand designer, 135–137
stand contractor, 138, 144
States of Guernsey, 54
syndicate sessions, 43

teleprompter, 74, 87, 90
theme, 4, 8, 12, 30, 63
 evening, 37
 parties, 37
trade seminars, 8
training courses, 9, 167
translation, 105, 141
travel, 103
travel agents, 123, 124, 125, 128
'24-hour rate', 113, 114

unions, 134
 cards, 139
 non-union members, 139
universities, 41–42, 162

vaccinations, 128
VAT, 24, 25, 26, 27, 114
ventilation, 46, 107
venue, 2, 12
 decoration of, 46
 definition of, 41
 facilities, 46–47
 letters of confirmation, 49, 51, 128
 selecting a suitable, 40–55, 151, 165
 site visit, 45–51, 75, 113, 127
video, 9, 38, 56, 74
 projector, 74
 tapes, 90
Video Arts Limited, 142
visual aids, 90

workshop, 46

The contributors

**Barbara Cox, MInstM, MACE,
Director, Meetings World (1969) Group**
Barbara Cox joined the board of Meetings World in 1982 and is a director and company secretary. Her field of experience covers international relations, marketing and organising conferences, training seminars, exhibitions and trade missions in the United Kingdom and throughout 60 countries worldwide, and in addition has also worked on specific assignments in areas as contrasting as Canada, Czechoslovakia, German Federal Republic, India, Singapore, United States and Zambia.

In her last position, Barbara Cox acted for the official UK public relations office on behalf of the Directorate General of Tourism for Indonesia. Her activities combined communications within the travel trade and the general public, responsible for specialised promotions, cultural activities and arranging theatrical events. Also, she represented Indonesia on the ASEAN (Association of South East Asian Nations) Tourism Committee.

**Geoffrey Gray-Forton, MACE, MInstTT,
MInstM, FInstD, Chairman and managing director
of Meetings World (1969) Group (Meetings World
Ltd.)**
Geoffrey Gray-Forton is a Founder Member of ACE International (Association of Conference Executives); he is immediate past executive director of International Congress & Convention Association director of International Congress & Convention

Association (ICCA) and a member of MPI (Meeting Planners International). An Honorary Citizen of the City of Winnipeg, Canada. He was also given the Freedom of the City of Tucson, USA.

Geoffrey has acted as moderator at over 350 events including seminars devoted to incentive travel, training, finance, law, presentations, technology, special interest programmes. He is frequently invited to lecture at colleges, universities and association events worldwide.

A regular contributor to the meetings, exhibitions and business travel press, and is editorial consultant to Business Travel Weekly magazine. He is a regular broadcaster with the BBC and LBC on various subjects.

Geoffrey Gray-Forton is the author of *The Conference Business and Travel Trade* book.

Terry Pottinger,
Associate Director, Moorgate Group plc

Terry Pottinger joined the Moorgate Group in 1985 to head its Conferences and Incentives Division. Highly skilled in the field of organising conventions, seminars and other incentive campaigns, Pottinger has worked for 20 years in the field of sales and marketing organising conferences. His speciality in the insurance industry is of particular reference to Moorgate's financial services clients.

The Moorgate Group was founded in 1977 and offers specialist financial marketing consultancy services to a broad range of companies in the financial services field. In addition to Conferences and Incentives, these services cover a wide range from product origination and development, through marketing consultancy, to direct mail, advertising, design and public relations.